Perfidious Albion

WILLIAM MCGURN is the Washington bureau chief of *National Review*. He previously spent five years with the editorial page of the *Wall Street Journal*, first in Brussels and then in Hong Kong. While in Hong Kong, he edited a volume on the first draft of the proposed post-1997 constitution, *Basic Law, Basic Questions: The Debate Continues*. He is also the author of a monograph on terrorism called *Terrorist or Freedom Fighter*, published by the London-based Institute for European Defence and Strategic Studies.

McGurn holds a B.A. in philosophy from the University of Notre Dame and an M.A. in communications from Boston University. He has returned to Hong Kong on reporting trips several times, and his articles on the colony have been published in *Newsweek*, *Esquire*, the *Far Eastern Economic Review*, *The American Spectator*, *The Spectator* (of London), the *National Catholic Register*, the *Washington Post*, the *South China Morning Post*, the *Los Angeles Times*, and elsewhere.

PERFIDIOUS ALBION

THE ABANDONMENT OF HONG KONG 1997

WILLIAM McGURN
Foreword by William F. Buckley, Jr.

ETHICS AND PUBLIC POLICY CENTER

Library of Congress Cataloging-in-Publication Data

McGurn, William.
Perfidious albion : the abandonment of Hong Kong, 1997 /
William McGurn ; foreword by William F. Buckley, Jr.
p.   cm.
Includes bibliographical references and index.
1. Hong Kong—Politics and government.   2. United States—
Emigration and immigration—Government policy.   3. Hong
Kong—Emigration and immigration.   I. Title.
DS796.H757M35   1991   951.2505—dc20   91–30675 CIP

ISBN 0–89633–162–8 (cloth : alk. paper)

 # 24319215

Distributed by arrangement with:
National Book Network
4720 Boston Way
Lanham, MD 20706

3 Henrietta Street
London WC2E 8LU England

All Ethics and Public Policy Center books are produced on acid-free paper. The paper used in this publication meets the minimum requirements of American National Standard for Information Sciences—Permanence of Paper for Printed Library Materials, ANSI Z39.48–1984.   ⊗ ™

Ethics and Public Policy Center
1015 Fifteenth Street N.W.
Washington, D.C. 20005
(202) 682–1200

To Joan and Angela,
that I may be proved wrong
about their future

Contents

Foreword

WILLIAM F. BUCKLEY, JR.

T HIS BOOK will both inform and mystify. We have all
known, more or less, that in 1997 Hong Kong will cease
to be a colony of Great Britain and that things will therefore
be different. But the developments leading to the upcoming
transformation have not been widely pondered, and nowhere
as succinctly as in these pages, by a young and gifted American
journalist who spent years in Asia and, as he puts it, fell in
love with Hong Kong. This is a romantic disease, I happen to
know, that hits quite a few people. It is under the circumstances extraordinary to find oneself asking the question:
What will happen to the people who have fallen in love with
Hong Kong or who, even if it is not an affair of the heart,
have lived and worked there for so many years, creating an
economic and demographic miracle that is the wonder of the
world? The author of this book, and those with foreign
passports, can under gentle auspices get over their love affair
with Hong Kong. Others can't.

We know only what will not happen to those people in
Hong Kong who elect to leave. They cannot go to Great
Britain. This is an extraordinary fact. We are dealing with 3.2
million human beings who have a British passport whose
meaning is, well, reduced to nothing at all: a curio, so to

speak, advising curious immigration inspectors of the background of the passport-holder.

So where else will they go? This is a problem that has confronted Asians for a very long time. When I was first in that part of the world (1962) the question was everywhere being asked, Where are the overseas Chinese who decline life under Mao Tse-tung to go? In fact, I asked the question of Chiang Kai-shek that year in an interview, and his answer was morally correct and politically evasive. What he said was that "room" had to be made for all Chinese fleeing oppression, but that just how they would be accommodated was a matter for diplomatic negotiation, but in any event didn't matter in the long run because—in the long run—mainland China would be liberated from the Chinese oppressors and everyone could go home. I had been sufficiently briefed to understand the meaning of the Generalissimo's statement, which was, "They can't come to Taiwan. They are not wanted here."

Now the assumptions, early on in the discussions between the British and the Chinese, were not common assumptions. In the early 1980s Mao was dead, yes, and the Gang of Four were sequestered, and economic opportunities were opening up in China, where perestroika (if not glasnost) had raised its inquisitive head. No doubt when British diplomatic papers are studied years from now we will see that the British were moved by great optimism, it being our legacy to assume that increased economic freedom would bring increased political freedom—which is often the case.

The Chinese, however—as Mr. McGurn reminds us in his introduction—engaged in attempting to right a wrong they carry as a suppurating wound to the pride of the Middle Kingdom: the colonization of Hong Kong after the Opium Wars. As far as the Chinese were concerned, when the discussions were begun about what would happen after 1997, ninety-nine years after the British consolidated their toehold in China, the question was one of historical rectification. Once a different future for Hong Kong was acknowledged as a question before the table, the British departure from Hong Kong was inevitable. The Chinese negotiators, affecting a common interest in the future of a distinctive Hong Kong, made such concessions as the British insisted upon, but in the ensuing months and years it became plain that the 1984 Sino-British Joint Declaration, far from proceeding under bilateral sponsorship, was becoming, little by little, an instrument in the hands of the Chinese by which they registered their determination to do everything they chose to do. The original accord looked forward to a Hong Kong with its own institutions, fashioned, after so many generations, by its unique experience. But time after time, where there was a dispute, the British yielded, giving life to the Chinese postulate that, really, it is not the business of Great Britain, let alone other countries, what the political arrangements are in China after 1997. And if "convergence" leads to humdrum totalitarian life, that is not the proper concern of foreign powers.

What astonishes Mr. McGurn, and stimulates in the reader a common concern, is, Just why has the whole thing been so mismanaged? The British had plenty of time to learn from the experience of Taiwan. If the subject of Taiwan came up, the powers in Peking were required to react with explosive resentment. For a while Mao was even bombing the islands of Quemoy and Matsu on odd days, more or less to give percussive resonance to his determination, if not to assert sovereignty, at least to claim it.

But as time went on the West learned that all we really needed to do—and this was done in 1972 at the Nixon détente—was to assert a theoretical formality that was in no sense different when spoken in Peking than when spoken in Taipei. That formality (formalism, really) was that Taiwan and mainland China were a single nation. As long as this was said, it turned out not greatly to matter that they were run as two very different nations.

What if the British has said that yes, Hong Kong was a part of China, but that historical events absolutely irreversible in character had sponsored a different culture in Hong Kong, a distinct culture, not one in which self-rule was the workaday political process but one in which there were rules, and independent courts, and maximum freedoms of property, and commerce, and movement; and that Great Britain had the responsibility to stand by a situation it had midwived—yes, what if?

Mr. McGurn reminds us that Great Britain has a relatively minor economic interest in Hong Kong, that therefore to make such an assertion would have been so to speak an international act of duty. But the assumption is that it would not have been seriously challenged by Deng Xiaoping, in particular if the historical abrasion were given balm enough to handle the problem of face. The British interest in Hong Kong is historical and administrative. By far the heaviest economic stake in Hong Kong is American. It is we who stand to lose the most commercially. Given the special relationship we have with Great Britain, we might have persuaded the government of Mrs. Thatcher to a higher pitch of resistance, citing British pride, historical responsibilities, and U.S. commercial interests. These might have combined to make the British insist on China's sticking to arrangements whose transcendent purpose is of course to guarantee to almost six million Asians the continuing advantages of a free life, in such conditions (improved by a generation of success) as prevailed in Shanghai up until that awful day in May 1949, so evocatively recaptured by Mr. McGurn, when old Shanghai slipped under the bamboo curtain.

The primacy of the doctrine of self-rule has been given a great deal of life in recent times, and the question will arise with mounting urgency, Is Hong Kong properly speaking nothing more than a satellite of China? Is there no meaning at all to its spectacular accomplishments, to its distinctive culture, to the ripeness with which it might take on self-rule? Martin Lee may just emerge as the Boris Yeltsin of Hong Kong, drawing international attention to the fate of Hong Kong under existing schedules. The eloquent Mr. Lee is off to exactly the right start, having been denounced by the Communist government as a "counter-revolutionary," which puts him in a class with the heroes of Eastern Europe and the Soviet Union who are now governing those countries.

This volume is worth not only reading but contemplating. It is not yet 1997. There is always the possibility that the old Maoist mandarinate will fall apart and that the events of Tiananmen Square will prove to be merely a prolonged version of the August 1991 putsch in Moscow. But if that doesn't happen, what else might happen? Will we see creative diplomacy, exercised by the British with American help, to prevent us from merely standing by for the greatest renewal of boat people in our time? Much hangs on how seriously this serious book is received.

William F. Buckley, Jr., is the editor-at-large of National Review.

Acknowledgments

THERE are many people without whose help this book would not have been possible. Space limitations preclude me from naming them all, but in particular I should like to thank the Ethics and Public Policy Center—George Weigel, who asked me to do it; Bob Royal, who followed up on it; and Carol Griffith, who put the whole thing together. In addition special mention should go to Frank Ching and John Walden for reading the draft and giving me their corrections and addenda. Any mistakes that remain are purely of my own making.

Martin Lee's office was most helpful. Tom Boasberg helped answer some tricky legal questions. And the ever efficient Joan Tong burned up the fax lines with whatever obscure document I asked her to locate. My thanks too to the officers of the Government Information Services. They must have known the drift the book was taking but never failed to nail down a fact when asked. Bud Williams and John Kamm at the American Chamber of Commerce in Hong Kong were especially helpful in regard to the last chapter. George Hicks provided some key clippings. And finally I should like to thank the writer of the foreword, William F. Buckley, Jr., a man whose frequent acts of kindness toward other writers generally go unmentioned.

I should also include a note about the rendering of Chinese names into English. For the most part I have used the pinyin system. But in a few places and names—e.g., Canton, Peking, Chiang Kai-shek—I have retained the older, more familiar form. In this, as in everything else, I could count on the help of innumerable friends and associates.

Individually these people contributed in various ways, here providing some desperately needed bit of information, there correcting a potential misimpression. Together their good cheer helped prevent even the dullest of tasks from degenerating into a solitary chore. My deepest appreciation and best wishes go with them always.

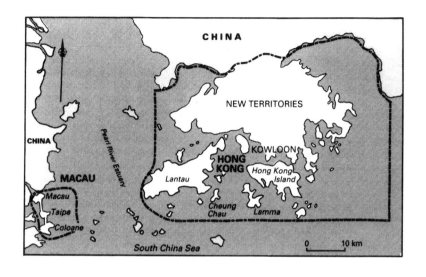

Reprinted by permission of the publisher, Prentice Hall Press, a Division of Simon & Schuster, New York, from *The Real Guide—Hong Kong and Macau*, by Jules Brown and Helen Lee (© 1991 by Jules Brown and Helen Lee).

Chronology

1841–42	Britain occupies Hong Kong Island as a result of its victory in the First Opium War; possession is formalized in the first of what China calls "the unequal treaties," the Treaty of Nanking.
1860	Second Opium War ends. Under the first Convention of Peking, China cedes part of Kowloon peninsula and Stonecutters Island, enhancing Hong Kong's size and security.
1898	The New Territories are added to Hong Kong under the second Convention of Peking. This time the land is not ceded outright but leased for 99 years—i.e., to 1997.
1900	Boxer Rebellion in China.
1911	Manchu dynasty overthrown in China; republic established.
1925–26	Nationalist fervor grows in Hong Kong. A general strike and boycott express popular indignation at the privileged status of foreigners.
1941–45	Japanese occupy Hong Kong.
1949	Communists capture the mainland, and Chiang Kai-shek flees to Taiwan. Peking seals the border with Hong Kong.
1951	U.N.-imposed trade embargo on China deprives Hong Kong of its single most important trading partner.
1952	Riots in Kowloon.

1950s-
mid-60s

Immigrants from the People's Republic of China flood into Hong Kong, almost doubling the population.

1967

Cultural Revolution spills over into Hong Kong. There are riots against British rule.

1972

China tells the U.N. to remove Hong Kong from its list of colonial territories: Hong Kong is to be considered sovereign Chinese soil.

1977

The senior PRC official responsible for Hong Kong says its status will not change until the issue of Taiwan has been resolved.

1979

The Hong Kong governor, Sir Murray MacLehose, travels to Peking and raises the question of 1997. Deng Xiaoping says China is satisfied with the status quo but will be forced to retake Hong Kong if Britain presses the issue.

1979-81

Britain continues to press China for an agreement on Hong Kong's post-1997 future.

1981

A new Nationality Act divides British citizenship into three categories. Hong Kong British passport-holders —now to be called British Dependent Territories Citizens—do not have the right of abode in Britain, unlike their counterparts in the colonies of Gibraltar and the Falklands.

1982

Formal Sino-British negotiations begin. Prime Minister Margaret Thatcher visits Peking and upsets her hosts by insisting on the inviolability of the treaties ceding Hong Kong to Britain.

1984

July: The government publishes a Green Paper. Public comment is invited on proposals "to develop progressively a system of government the authority for which is firmly rooted in Hong Kong, which is able to represent authoritatively the views of the people of Hong Kong, and which is more directly accountable to the people of Hong Kong."

September: The draft agreement of the Sino-British Joint Declaration is initialed.

November: The government publishes a White Paper, "The Further Development of Representative Government in Hong Kong." Although it does not promise direct elections in 1988, the paper acknowledges that "the bulk of public response from all sources suggested a cautious approach with a gradual start by introducing a very small number of directly elected members in 1988 and building up to a significant number of directly elected members by 1997."

December: Mrs. Thatcher returns to Peking, this time to sign the Sino-British Joint Declaration establishing the terms for the return of Hong Kong to China.

1985   *May*: Britain and China ratify the Joint Declaration.

November: The director of the New China News Agency in Hong Kong, Peking's unofficial representative, makes a veiled accusation against Britain for violating the terms of the Joint Declaration by attempting to introduce political reforms in Hong Kong.

1987   *May*: The government publishes a Green Paper that, unlike the 1984 Green Paper, does not advocate any specific political reform and instead invites public comment on a number of options. A Survey Office set up to gather these views later commissions two polls on direct elections.

November: Hong Kong governor Sir David Wilson denies a brain drain, insisting that "the level of emigration has been much the same as it is now for more than twenty years."

1988   *February*: The government publishes a White Paper, "The Development of Representative Government: The Way Forward" that announces a number of political revisions. The most controversial is the decision to put off direct elections until 1991, after China has approved the Basic Law. Protestors burn copies of the White Paper outside the Central Government Offices.

April: The governor admits the brain drain is a "problem" and says his government will investigate. / The first draft of the Basic Law is released.

October: In an effort to stem the brain drain, the American Chamber of Commerce sends a delegation to Peking to argue for increased freedoms in the Basic Law.

December: Some 5,000 march in a pro-democracy rally outside the New China News Agency in Hong Kong.

1989   *February*: China releases the second draft of the Basic Law.

May: The people of Hong Kong hold public marches —unprecedented in scale—in support of the Peking Spring in Tiananmen Square.

June 3–4: The massacre in Tiananmen Square. More than a million Hong Kong people take to the streets in peaceful protest.

June 5: In a policy statement about "current events in China," Sir Geoffrey Howe, British foreign secretary, says Britain "could not easily contemplate a massive new immigration commitment" to Hong Kong.

October: The governor announces $16 billion port-and-airport development upgrades to try to restore international confidence in the colony.

December: The British begin the forcible repatriation of Vietnamese refugees in Hong Kong back to Hanoi. As a result, world sympathy for Hong Kong is greatly reduced.

1990   *February*: London and Peking agree to limit the number of directly elected members of Hong Kong's Legislative Council to a third in 1995–99.

April: The British announce a package of 50,000 passports to select Hong Kong families. / The National People's Congress in Peking approves and ratifies the Basic Law, which pro-democracy forces say is incompatible with the 1984 Joint Declaration.

June: Chinese authorities continue to attack Britain's plan for a new airport, fearing that the project will be used to strip Hong Kong of its reserves. The airport becomes a major political issue and a test of Britain's commitment to its colony.

1991   *July*: Britain and China issue a Memorandum of Understanding concerning the airport, giving China a say in the awarding of contracts.

September: Pro-democracy candidates led by Martin Lee win all but 2 of the 18 seats contested (out of the Legislative Council's 60 seats). No pro-China candidate wins.

November: The British force back another group of Vietnamese boat people, in an effort to empty the camps in 2–3 years.

Introduction

O N THE main wall of my apartment in Washington hangs a watercolor of Shanghai. The view looks north along the Huangpu River promenade called the Bund, past the Customs House to the 1930s art deco Bank of China and the old Cathay (now Peace) Hotel, where Noel Coward stayed and wrote *Private Lives* when he was pent up with influenza. I bought the painting on a visit to Shanghai in 1989, attracted by the New Yorkish aura of metropolis punctuated by a hint of the East in the way the bank's blue-tiled roof, some sixteen stories above it all, turns up at the corners—as if the Empire State Building had been given a Chinese cap.

The urban sophistication of this scene makes it quite unlike traditional Chinese paintings, with their pastoral settings suggestive of stillness and contentment. The contrast is appropriate here, because Shanghai rose to prominence in China as something of a contradiction. Like Hong Kong today, Shanghai was an unabashedly cosmopolitan city situated in one of the world's most provincial national cultures. The mix proved propitious, combining the best and worst of Occident and Orient into something greater than the sum of its parts. And after the city fell to the Communists in May 1949, many of its leading industrialists, now penniless refugees in Hong Kong, breathed a little of Shanghai's soul into that dusty crown colony, transforming it in turn into a world-rank city.

Both places owed their birth to Britain's victory in the First

1

Opium War. But whereas Hong Kong was a British colony under the British flag, Shanghai was a treaty port under a variety of flags. Here Iraqi Jews rubbed shoulders with White Russians; British, American, French, and German traders competed for a share of the ever lucrative China market; Catholic priests and Protestant missionaries vied for the souls of the heathen populace; Chinese from all parts of the mainland lived crowded together in often unspeakable poverty; and misfits and adventurers from all ends of the earth found a corner they could call home. "Shanghai is not China," explains a 1934 travel guide to the city. "It is everything else under the sun, and, in population at least, is mostly Chinese, but it is not the real China."

To legions of expatriates, Shanghai was a place for cream cakes and macaroons down in the French concession, the jazz band at the Cathay, spectacular sales at the Sun Sun Department Store, singsong girls on Fuzhou Road, and, perhaps to atone for it all, Mass the next morning at the Jesuit cathedral. In the shadow of this expatriate community lived the overwhelming majority of the population, the Chinese, lured by the scent of opportunity. They might be wealthy *compradors*, or go-betweens for the large trading houses. But more common were the wretchedly poor, coolies who considered themselves fortunate if they managed to get their daily ration of rice, people who lived and worked in the alleyways that stank of human feces clogging open drains and, at times, of the emaciated corpses of Chinese who had died of hunger, overwork, or assassination. Although the sign outside the Public Gardens did not say, as folklore has it, "No Dogs or Chinese Allowed," it did list regulations one of which excluded Chinese and another of which prohibited dogs.

Still, for all its undeniable failings, Shanghai worked, in a way that no other Chinese city had done. What made it work was the happy marriage of Western law and the instinctive Chinese knack for commerce. To the revolutionaries who would eventually overrun Shanghai, the whole notion of International Settlements, with their own laws, courts, and police forces, was an affront to the dignity of the Middle Kingdom. Multitudes of their fellow countrymen, however, evidently preferred rule by the foreign devil to rule by their own, for from the outset Shanghai was a magnet for Chinese. And when the People's Army finally marched in, the businessmen vainly supposed then, as their sons in Hong Kong suppose today, that the Communists, like everyone else, couldn't do without them.

The resemblance to Hong Kong is not accidental. The Bank of China, whose picturesque building once graced the Shanghai skyline, now flaunts its soaring tower on the skyline of Hong Kong. The great Shanghai department stores, Wing On and Sincere, now cater to the people of Hong Kong, as do the old trading firms of Jardine Mattheson and Butterfield and Swire. Hong Kong's first families, the Kadoories, the Sassoons, the Lis, are dynasties transplanted from the north. Kelly and Walsh no longer print in Shanghai, but they do a thriving business selling books in Hong Kong. In Shanghai only the shells of its past remain, leaving the impression of a city suspended in time.

In retrospect, it seems baffling that savvy old Shanghailanders trusted Communist assurances, given the generally hardheaded outlook they had acquired from years of doing business in the Far East. Indeed, at the time, the U.S. Consul General in Shanghai, John Cabot, marveled that so many people who knew China so much better than he could actually rejoice as the red star was raised over the city. In Noel Barber's splendid account of those final days, *The Fall of Shanghai*, he captured the haughty indifference of Shanghai's population on the eve of Communist rule:

> Asia's greatest city, the fourth largest port in the world, it stood alone—not courageously, no bastion of stubborn

defiance, but in a strange way aloof, flaunting its unconcern for the future, as though its six million inhabitants had closed a collective eye to the civil war around them and were determined that, until the enemy reached the gates, the city would remain in all its glory, a last oasis of yesterday in the China of tomorrow.

In post-Tiananmen Hong Kong, such insouciance is no longer possible, inasmuch as the transition to Communist rule, to take place officially in 1997, has already begun to tell. It starts with the landscape. From its base in the central district of Hong Kong, the seventy-story Bank of China building, designed by I. M. Pei, completely dominates the city skyline. The bank is Communist-owned. Its main competitor, the British-owned Hong Kong and Shanghai Bank, has pulled out of Hong Kong. The skyscraper—the tallest building in Asia —is a stark reminder of China's forthcoming resumption of sovereignty over the colony. The city's Cantonese inhabitants refer to it as a *choi doh*, or knife, at Hong Kong's throat.

The bank tower was originally built as a sign equally of the mainland's confidence in Hong Kong's post-1997 future and its commitment to liberalization at home. But in the aftermath of June 4, 1989, the building was draped with a banner whose Chinese characters read "Blood Must Be Paid With Blood." For the Tiananmen massacre rocked Hong Kong to its capitalist core.

Partly this was business: over the past decade, as Peking has opened its doors, the economies of Hong Kong and the People's Republic of China have become intertwined, so that each now has a considerable stake in the other's fate. So long as reform continued on the mainland, the more optimistic (usually those who held foreign passports) took consolation in the "one country, two systems" formula enshrined in the 1984 Sino-British Joint Declaration that laid out the terms for the colony's handover to China. Today, however, the 5.8 million inhabitants of Hong Kong are all too conscious that in just six short years they too will be ruled by the government that set the People's Liberation Army on its own people.

To make matters worse, they know also that they can no longer count on the good faith of the colony's increasingly nominal sovereign, the United Kingdom. Initially the 1984 Joint Declaration, which set out the terms of the 1997 transfer of sovereignty from London to Peking, was met with high hopes, coupled as it was with official British pronouncements that representative government in Hong Kong would be installed and working well before the Union Jack was lowered for the last time. Yet in the years after Margaret Thatcher put her name to the document, her government implemented none of the promised reforms that might have given the agreement a fighting chance. The crowning blow was then foreign secretary Geoffrey Howe's statement in Commons just two days after the Tiananmen killings that Britain's door remained closed to all but a handful of its non-white passport-holders in Hong Kong.

In Hong Kong, the word "colony" was long ago purged from the official lexicon, but I use it consciously in this book, as a reminder of who wields authority and thus bears responsibility for what happens in the territory at least until 1997. To those outside Hong Kong, Tiananmen Square is sometimes thought to have sabotaged well-laid British plans for Hong Kong's future. In fact, Tiananmen Square has in a perverse way served British interests, if one reads these interests as getting out with a minimum of bother. However bad it made things for Hong Kong, Tiananmen Square provided the British with a convenient out: the claim that the process was moving along fine until China mucked it up. In June 1989 the barbarous resort to tanks and gunfire revealed the true face of the Chinese regime all around the globe. But the true face of Britain—whose embassy in Peking turned away Hong Kong British seeking protection during the bloody crackdown—remains largely hidden.

The idea that Hong Kong's present difficulties derive solely (or even mainly) from China and date from June 4, 1989, is so manifestly absurd that it is never raised inside the colony. Its province lies elsewhere, in the arena of foreign affairs, where it provides Britain with an intellectual fig leaf. And it has been particularly useful in the United States.

I have heard or read this rationale dozens of times since my return to the States from what had been my home in Hong Kong. Most blatant was its use at a breakfast meeting in New York, when John Major, then foreign secretary, flatly told a dozen or so reporters that there had been absolutely no crisis of confidence in the colony before Tiananmen Square. For a moment I thought I had heard incorrectly, and I requested a clarification. Mr. Major repeated his assertion, thus neatly absolving his government of any responsibility for what has gone so wrong in its prize possession.

The daily headlines in Hong Kong tell a different story. The *Asian Wall Street Journal* and the *Far Eastern Economic Review* were editorializing about the crisis facing Hong Kong as far back as 1985/86. In January 1988, the managing director of Bond International complained to a *South China Morning Post* reporter that "until the Government is able to make concrete decisions—not giving in to China—I don't know if confidence can be restored." In early 1988 Hong Kong's governor, Sir David Wilson, was conceding that the brain drain whose existence he had up to then vehemently denied was indeed a serious problem.

Just as telling were the little personal signs: the secretary who announced she was leaving for Australia; the friend who gave up a promising bank career to relocate in Canada; the little advertisements for immigration lawyers that began cropping up in the local classifieds. In good Hong Kong fashion, someone even found a way to make a profit out of the uncertainty by launching a magazine called *The Emigrant*.

All this is by way of introducing the central argument of

this book: that the crisis in Hong Kong owes itself first to Britain and to China only second; that Britain has deliberately thwarted developments that might have shored up Hong Kong; that at least one major decision, the refusal to give its passport-holders the right to emigrate to Britain, has been based on racial considerations; and that, instead of building up Hong Kong institutions to withstand the buffeting they will have to take under even the best of circumstances come 1997, the government has by default allowed China to determine the shape of these institutions. The world saw this formalized in the 1991 resolution of the Sino-British dispute over the proposed airport, when China was given a say in all major decisions.

My argument extends to America: that, as perhaps the largest foreign investor in the colony, the United States has, next to the people of Hong Kong themselves, the greatest stake in its future and consequently ought to assume a more active role in shaping developments there, even at the risk of upsetting Britain, which has less and less of a stake each year. The United States cannot "save" Hong Kong, but it can, as I note in the last chapter, contribute to the health and prosperity of the colony not only through its immigration policy but also by actions that treat Hong Kong as an entity separate from the PRC; some members of the American Chamber of Commerce in Hong Kong are urging the United States to adopt an act that would make this practice more explicit. In late 1991, Senator Mitch McConnell introduced precisely such a bill, the U.S.–Hong Kong Policy Act, supported by colleagues as diverse as Connie Mack and Paul Simon.

What would best serve America's interests would be for Hong Kong to remain as it is. Inasmuch as the probability of this recedes with every passing day, the next best thing is to get as many as possible of Hong Kong's people to its own shores, so that they will use their talents and energy to advance American rather than Australian or Canadian interests. Let me be understood: I wish exile on no man. I only remind a nation largely descended from the hopeful multitudes of Ellis and Angel islands that we have historically been graced to recognize blessings where others see only burdens.

None of this is meant to downplay China's contributions to Hong Kong's woes; nor is it to deny the effect its brutish actions at home have had on confidence in Hong Kong's future. It is to suggest, however, that naïveté about China's true nature has by and large been confined to those expatriates and officials whose foreign passports mean they will never have to submit to Peking's dominion. The Hong Kong Chinese have had few such illusions. Most, after all, are either refugees from the PRC or the children of such refugees. The suppositions upon which the Joint Declaration rested required a Western trust in formal legalisms, not to mention a certain personal distance, that Hong Kong people simply never had. Yet through it all they retained a remarkable faith that the British would somehow see them through.

This was largely the situation back in January 1988, when early one Sunday morning Hong Kong columnist and author Frank Ching, Legislative Council member Martin Lee, and I gathered at the Kowloon home of economist and long-time Hong Kong resident George Hicks. Our intention was to propose a book that would track the implementation of the Joint Declaration from its inception up to the first draft of the Basic Law, the mainland-drafted mini-constitution for post-1997 Hong Kong, which was to be released that coming April. Various authors would discuss the impact of the Basic Law on every aspect of Hong Kong life, from economics and civil rights to religion and freedom of the press. A more pessimistic group than the four of us meeting in the Hicks living room would have been hard to find. As it turned out, even we underestimated the degree to which the colony would continue to diverge from the 1984 agreement and the speed with which disillusionment would grow.

Today the final draft of the Basic Law has been approved by Peking, and the grim contours of post-1997 Hong Kong are already visible. The Basic Law virtually cancels out the key provisions of the Joint Declaration—the "high degree of autonomy" and a legislature "constituted by elections." It also weights future political developments toward the PRC, making it unlikely that Hong Kong will ever get the democracy promised in 1984. Ironically, the early drafts of the law released *before* Tiananmen Square were even worse; clearly, China's bad intentions toward Hong Kong did not begin on June 4, 1989.

In this light, the decision to shelve a program to institute representative government in Hong Kong before 1997 has a rather malevolent cast. At a private dinner for Martin Lee during his spring 1990 visit to Washington, a British embassy official explained this decision to a group of editors by saying it would not be "prudent" for Britain to go ahead with such reforms against China's wishes, whatever Hong Kong sentiment might be. "Is that not our decision, our risk, to take?" Mr. Lee countered. The official retreated into silence. And I have yet to hear a convincing rejoinder.

To be sure, most of those who have run Hong Kong so well up to these critical last few years retain deep misgivings about democracy. Singapore's prime minister Lee Kuan Yew went so far as to blame the Tiananmen massacre and the turmoil in Hong Kong on a foreign-instigated campaign for a democratic Hong Kong. (Mr. Lee, quick to condemn "outside interference" in his state, by which he means foreign-owned papers that try to cover Singapore's politics, seems to have few qualms about interfering in Hong Kong's politics.) For their part many American conservatives, mindful of the havoc wreaked by Wilsonian crusades in the past, view calls for democracy with suspicion.

A call for prudence in the matter of democracy-building is perfectly legitimate. All too often, however, such warnings tend to elevate circumspection from an operational principle to an ideological authorization for the status quo. Where people have demonstrated their desire for democracy, and have reached a level of development commensurate with the responsibilities that representative government demands of its citizens, is not the better course to impress upon these people the exacting requirements for democracy to work rather than dismiss their desires for the freedoms so cherished in the West? It seems to me that this is not only advisable but imperative in the fact of a Communist alternative.

Conservatives and liberals alike have been guilty of viewing democracy solely in terms of a vote, confusing a mere mechanism with an overall process of self-rule. The ordered liberty upon which democracy can be built requires a solid middle class, an independent judiciary, respect for the sanctity of contracts and private property. These requirements may be more difficult to establish than the democracy they presage. Yet Hong Kong more than meets them, having long experience of both common law and the enterprise it makes possible.

In the past one might have pointed to Hong Kong as an example of a place that got along splendidly without democracy. But the crunch it faces today dramatically illustrates just how unprepared those unschooled in self-rule are in times of political crisis. Hong Kong underwent social and economic transformation under British colonial rule. The failure to match these achievements with commensurate political institutions rooted in and reflecting the people of Hong Kong has kept the colony dependent upon Britain and thus in danger of seeing all these achievements wither with Britain's departure in 1997. Hong Kong's tragedy—a legacy of a benign and well-intentioned colonialism—was to have failed to appreciate its own special identity until too late.

One need not be a thoroughgoing cynic to note how convenient this has been for both Peking and London. Any government of the people, by the people, and for the people of Hong Kong would present an insurmountable obstruction to the blueprint they have laid out for post-1997 Hong Kong. By no means would democracy guarantee a brighter future. But it would for the first time give those who have to live with that future some say in determining its shape.

Discomfiting premonitions of Hong Kong's likely future abound in Shanghai. Like Hong Kong today, Shanghai in its heyday represented a remarkable meeting of East and West, what T. L. Tsim has characterized as an essentially European commonweal with strong American influences. For all its double standards and irksome extraterritoriality, Shanghai nonetheless attracted a significant number of Chinese who preferred to be second-class citizens in a settlement of even limited opportunity rather than full members of a tempestuous world run by their own that offered them so little. When the foreign devils left, the magic left with them.

How cheerless is Shanghai today! The jazz band still plays every evening in the Cathay, but the bass has a nasty crack and the table linen is soiled. The Wing On is still there, only now it is called No. 10 Department Store and hasn't had a fresh coat of paint in decades. New hotels like the Sheraton, Hilton, and Mandarin have shot up amid the older tenements crammed with iron poles full of laundry; their whiteness makes them stand out awkwardly amid the collectivist drab, like too-new sneakers on a ten-year-old boy. On the electric tram lines, masses of unsmiling workers press their faces against grimy windows, and on the main thoroughfares descendants of Shanghai's cosmopolitan business class accost the now rare foreigner in the desperate hope of practicing their English. Most depressing of all was the shiny polyester suit I came upon in the window of The Western Style Suit Company on the old Avenue Joffre, a charming street that was once the Savile Row of the Far East. Shanghai has become a museum, not because it has been preserved but because it has been neglected.

I wonder: Will this be the same reaction of some old China hand some twenty or thirty years hence revisiting the Hong Kong that I knew, and came to love, as my second home? Is it all that hard to imagine the lobby of the Mandarin Oriental stained and tatty? The Foreign Correspondents' Club shuttered and abandoned? Or the smartly dressed Hong Kong office girls recast in the lumpen jackets and schoolmarmish outfits of their mainland cousins? In the lobby of the old Palace Hotel on Nanking Road, I was startled to find a copy of a glossy book on Tiananmen Square offered for sale; when I asked for a look, it turned out to be an official publication, ponderously entitled *The Truth About the Beijing Turmoil*. It is no comfort to recollect that Shanghai's own death came about not by a quick gunshot but through slow strangulation. In *Mouldering Pearl: Hong Kong at the Crossroads*, Felix Patrikeeff put it this way:

> Shanghai is *still* the most important, most productive centre of trade and commerce in China. And it is still as crowded and bustling as it was when it was dominated by capitalists. At the same time, its tall elegant buildings suggest that it has been frozen in its heyday, as if it has become a shell. There is no longer that intangible feeling of a productive intermingling of East and West. Hong Kong too may find itself inheriting this twilight status: changed from a window on the world to just another Chinese city.

As one old Shanghai survivor, kept under city arrest for ten years after the Communists arrived, told me in the resplendent lobby of Hong Kong's Peninsula Hotel, "All the experts told us they'd never touch Shanghai. Don't kid yourself. It's all built on sand."

In such a world, hope becomes an act of will. Just as no one ever expected the degree to which Margaret Thatcher, the self-styled Iron Lady, would kowtow before Deng Xiaoping, few could have predicted that Hong Kong's deliverance may yet come from China itself. The crackdown on Tiananmen Square was not the end of the story but the beginning: for five glorious weeks the Chinese people, joined by their kin in Hong Kong, poured into the square to show where they stood and raised a Statue of Liberty to show where they wanted to go.

When Mrs. Thatcher held a press conference in 1984 to announce the Joint Declaration, a Hong Kong reporter asked her about the morality of delivering more than five million people into Communist hands. At the time the Iron Lady dismissed the questioner as "a solitary exception" to prevailing opinion. But six years later this same reporter became one of the colony's first elected representatives, winning a seat as an outspoken critic of both the British and the Chinese government. She was joined by seventeen others, all but one of whom are avowed democrats and none of whom is pro-China. Led by Martin Lee, whom Bill Buckley correctly describes as a Chinese Yeltsin, they give Hong Kong people what they most need at this critical juncture: a voice.

Of course, what kind of Hong Kong the world will have in 1997 now depends on what kind of China the world will have in 1997. Today the aged patriarchs of a discredited ideology have won, if that is the right word. But the China of tomorrow may yet have more to do with those now clanking their chains in prison, hiding out in exile, or taking their democratically determined seats in Hong Kong's Legislative Council, than with those who, for the moment, sit triumphant atop the bloody heap. In these people reposes the last distant hope that Hong Kong will never become "just another Chinese city."

1

Beyond Suzie Wong

IT WAS 1957, it was a chance ride on the Star Ferry, and it was Hong Kong. He was an aspiring painter named Robert Lomax. Her name was Suzie Wong, and though it turned out she was fibbing a bit about her honor—"I proud to be good girl," she insisted — in Hollywood's nice, 1950s, black-and-white sort of way he fell for her anyway.

More than three decades after Nancy Kwan first shimmied across the screen in *The World of Suzie Wong*, American notions of Britain's prize crown colony remain mired in this film adaptation of the Richard Mason novel. This is the Hong Kong of corrugated tin huts perched uneasily on muddy hillsides, of appalling sweatshops packed with ancient women toiling in dangerous conditions beside their grandchildren, of a harbor clogged with old-fashioned Chinese junks in full patchy sail, and, of course, of comely bargirls like Suzie wheedling drinks from unsuspecting sailors in the seedy Wanchai district. It is a city of greedy robber barons, starched Englishmen and their horrid wives, penniless escapees from the Communist mainland just across the border, and masses and masses of faceless Chinese living atop one another in unspeakable squalor. It is, in short, a Dickensian set painted in the exotic colors of the Far East.

This picture was never wholly accurate even in its own time; today it's patently absurd. In little more than a generation; tiny Hong Kong has leapt from sampans and sedan chairs to

15

hydrofoils and jumbo jets. The corrugated tin rooftops of those desperate shacks have given way to land-reclamation projects and sleek new skyscrapers. Women's slit-sheath silk *cheongsams* are not seen much outside the lounges of the world-famous luxury hotels like the Peninsula and the Mandarin Oriental. On Queens Road Central the occasional coolie threads his way through the crowded streets with a crushing load carried in two baskets strung from a pole across his shoulders, but a more likely sight is a well-tailored Chuppie—Chinese Yuppie —checking in with his broker or his mistress on a cellular phone. The only rickshaws are outside the Star Ferry downtown, where their owners lie in wait for tourists willing to pay for a taste of old Hong Kong.

The numbers alone tell much of the story. The 5.8 million inhabitants of Hong Kong, all but a fraction of them ethnic Chinese, are jammed into only 413.5 square miles of mostly inhospitable land. This makes their home one of the most densely populated places on earth, at 14,026 people per square mile. Despite this, and despite the complete lack of natural resources (it depends on neighboring China for water, for example), Hong Kong has evolved into the world's eleventh-largest trading power, its third-busiest financial center (after New York and London), and its largest port. The people of Hong Kong enjoy the highest income in Asia next to Japan's (and an arguably higher standard of living than the Japanese, given the distortions of an overvalued yen), and half of them live in government housing.

Altogether some 242,700 companies vie for business in the colony, including seventy-six of the world's top one hundred banks. Hong Kong is the world's largest exporter of toys, has more Rolls Royces per capita than any other place on earth, consumes the fourth-largest amount of brandy in the world in absolute terms, and boasts one of the smallest unemployment rates—1.7 per cent in 1990. Between 1979 and 1989 its gross domestic product grew at an average 9 per cent, twice the rate for the rest of the world. And this thriving capitalism is not the jealously guarded domain of a tiny clique of satisfied *tai-pans*, or corporate chieftains: of the colony's 17,340 taxi cabs, for example, all but a thousand or so are individually owned.

Everywhere the place sweats with commerce. In sharp contrast to the picturesque languor of much of the rest of the developing world, modern Hong Kong is a Brueghelesque jumble of high-rise apartment blocks, glass skyscrapers, innumerable mom-and-pop shops, supersize shopping malls, and ritzy hotels. On almost every square inch of the colony people are busily selling to one another. Street hawkers crowd alleyways with all manner of wares. Italian, French, Vietnamese, American, German, Mexican, Cantonese, Burmese, Indian, Thai, Szechuan, and Korean restaurants cater to every conceivable taste; tailors measure and fit clients of every nationality and race; furniture shops along Queens Road East churn out custom-made rosewood and rattan, while factories no larger than the average bedroom busily fill orders from customers around the world for everything from pencils and picture frames to microchips.

The result is a per capita income for Hong Kong people one and a half times that of their cousins on Taiwan and thirty times that on the mainland, an income higher than that in some West European countries and rapidly closing the gap on Mother England herself. Foreigners sometimes are repelled by the grosser spectacles of the Hong Kong rich enjoying their wealth, but the marriage of British law and Chinese resourcefulness has proved fruitful for those on the bottom no less than those on the top. "There are few places in the world where such a large proportion of the population is at least doing what it wants to do, where it wants to be," writes historian Jan Morris.[1] Even those who are most repulsed by the undisguised pursuit of profit confess to finding Hong Kong oddly seductive.

Of course, it wasn't always finance and fax machines. The

birth of Hong Kong was a seamy affair, tainted by the substance the Chinese called "foreign mud" and the British saw as a means to settle their balance of payments: opium.

Arrival of the Europeans

For centuries the European powers had tried to open China to foreign commerce, but until the nineteenth century such trade as existed was confined to Canton and then only at certain well-defined seasons and under maddening restrictions. In 1793 Lord George Macartney led a mission to the Chinese court in Peking, where he petitioned the emperor Qianlong to allow Britain to establish an embassy as a prelude to reducing tariffs and easing restrictions on the onerous trade system. The emperor's reply was brief and to the point. "We have never valued ingenious articles, nor do we have the slightest need of your country's manufactures," he told King George III in a celebrated letter. "Therefore, O king, as regards your request to send someone to remain at the capital, while it is not in harmony with the regulations of the Celestial Empire we also feel very much that it is of no advantage to your country."[2] Macartney was rebuffed on all points. His only small victory was to have exempted himself from performing the *kowtow*, the ceremonial display of deference a visitor shows upon admission to the royal presence; the full kowtow calls for pressing one's head and knees to the floor nine times.

This stubborn indifference to the allures of the outside world characterized almost all aspects of China's foreign relations, for the simple reason that the Chinese regarded their country as the one repository of civilization on earth—the Middle Kingdom between heaven and earth—and those not under its sway as by definition barbarians. No ambassadors resided in the Chinese capital because China would not accept other nations as equals. The commercial traders they did allow were ever reminded that they were there on the emperor's sufferance, not for any mutual benefit. Thus Western commerce with China was limited to the "factories" (actually, large warehouses) at Canton, a large deep-water port on the Pearl River. Traders were permitted to be there only from October to May and had to leave their families in the nearby Portuguese colony of Macau. They were forbidden to enter the city or to learn the Chinese language, and they were subject to the whims of local officials. Since the foreign barbarians were beneath even the lowest Chinese, they were not fit to address the local mandarins directly but were forced to petition the Chinese monopoly of businesses called the Co-Hong. Thus did the authorities hope to limit and regulate contact with the outside world.

But the traders were not easily daunted. The apparently unlimited market for Chinese silks, porcelains, and particularly tea held out the possibility of vast profits if only commerce could be regularized.

Enter Opium

In addition to the bureaucratic difficulties there was one other. Qianlong was not exaggerating when he wrote of China's lack of interest in foreign goods. This meant that the foreigners had to pay in silver, and the British Treasury was soon suffering from a huge net outflow of sterling. The British needed to find something they could sell to the Chinese. That something turned out to be opium, grown in British India. The Chinese had learned how to smoke opium mixed with tobacco, and the demand for the powder was evidently insatiable.

Although the Chinese government thought the drug harmful and banned traffic in it, the authorities were powerless to enforce their will. The incentives were just too strong: local officials turned a blind eye in exchange for a cut of the profits;

the opium dealers were better equipped and often more heavily armed than the government forces trying to suppress them; and Chinese as well as British merchants found opium sales wonderfully convenient. Almost all the leading entrepreneurs of the day trafficked in opium, including William Jardine (nicknamed "the iron-headed old rat" by the Chinese), whose trading company remains the most prominent firm in Hong Kong today. Some missionaries even saw in opium the key to introducing China to Christianity.

The Chinese, for their part, watched with alarm as opium imports grew. In the early eighteenth century imports had been about 200 chests a year, but by 1821 that figure had grown to 5,000 chests, and a decade later 16,500 chests. In 1833, in response to the pressure from the Free Traders gaining ascendancy in England, the East India Company lost its monopoly on trade, and the figures for opium jumped even higher, reaching 40,000 chests by 1839–40.[3] The result was that the flow of silver reversed itself, and now China, not Britain, found its reserves depleted.

The diplomatic situation only compounded the strains. Inasmuch as Britain had no relations with China, Her Majesty's representatives took the view that they were not bound to enforce the emperor's laws and so did not interfere with the British merchant ships carrying the narcotic. In 1834 the foreign secretary, Lord Palmerston, dispatched Lord Napier of Maristoun to be chief superintendent of trade at Canton; he was told to avoid antagonizing China and to try to establish direct relations with the government. But William Jardine and the other merchants wanted a showdown with Peking and egged Napier on. The British emissary then forced a confrontation by personally violating a number of the Chinese-imposed restrictions. The Chinese responded by curtailing all trade. Napier then had his justification for sending warships to Canton, but they were forced to withdraw. Suffering from fever, he died in Macau a few months later, having met with the same failure as many others before him.

But the stage was set for further confrontation, as the opium problem proliferated. The drug was now costing the Qing government in China a tenth of its revenue each year, and in March 1839 the emperor appointed an anti-opium reformer named Lin Zexu to the post of high commissioner for Canton. Lin set about his work almost immediately, informing the young Queen Victoria that "we mean to cut off this powerful drug forever." He took a similarly strong line with the foreign merchants based in Canton, where he began to arrest and execute those caught dealing in the substance. The showdown came when Lin ordered the *hongs*, or trading houses, to hand over all their opium, cutting off all food and water to the factories until the order was obeyed. After a six-week siege, Captain Charles Elliot, the new British superintendent of trade, handed over 20,283 chests of opium valued at three million pounds sterling. Lin had it all destroyed.

Elliot then withdrew to Macau and sent a report to the British government back home. Because the Portuguese did not want to get in the middle of a Sino-British squabble over opium, however, the British ships left Macau to anchor in the harbor of a small island off the south China coast named Hong Kong. When Commissioner Lin paid a visit to Macau with several hundred armed men, Elliot advised the British residents and their families to leave their homes there and seek refuge on the ships moored in Hong Kong. Lin subsequently followed up his previous orders with another notice cutting off all supplies to the British, to try to force them back to Canton under his authority. In the midst of all this H.M.S. *Volage* arrived in Hong Kong and attacked the Chinese forces blockading the stranded British families. Although Elliot did not want a fight—and was bitterly attacked for being too conciliatory toward the Chinese—Lin pressed his demands, and the captain ultimately responded by destroying the Chinese naval forces there.

In the meantime, London was growing more inclined to

get tough with Peking. Lord Palmerston wanted to set Sino-British trade straight once and for all, either through a commercial treaty that would guarantee fair trade or by acquiring some land that the British could then use as a base in the region, under British law and British regulations. Palmerston backed up this idea by dispatching a Royal Navy expeditionary force from India, and by June 1840 the first of the British warships had arrived in Canton.

The British Take Possession

This was the beginning of the First Opium War. The Chinese were no match for the Royal Navy, and after a few skirmishes negotiations began between Captain Elliot and the new Chinese commissioner, Qishan. Initially the commissioner resisted the British demands, and the talks did not resume until Elliot had again resorted to a show of force. On January 20, 1841, the two men reached an agreement called the Convention of Chuenpi—later repudiated by both governments—under which British firms would be reestablished in Canton and the island of Hong Kong ceded to Her Majesty. Six days later, a landing party raised the Union Jack at a spot named Possession Point. With this inauspicious start British Hong Kong was born.

At the time the British took control, Hong Kong's tiny population of about 3,650 was scattered over twenty villages and hamlets; another 2,000 or so fishermen lived on their boats. A ridge of mountains made farming next to impossible. The only thing to recommend the island was one great natural asset: a fine, sheltered harbor. It would be named Victoria, after the Queen. Under the Chuenpi agreement, although the colony would be ruled in accordance with British law, the local Chinese were to continue to enjoy rule by their own laws and customs, "every description of torture excepted."

Back home, Elliot was castigated for having been too soft.

Queen Victoria wrote to her uncle that "all we wanted might have been got, if it had not been for the unaccountably strange conduct of Charles Elliot . . . who completely disobeyed his instructions and *tried* to get the *lowest* terms he could."[4] Lord Palmerston was blunter still, dismissing the Queen's latest acquisition as "a barren island with hardly a house upon it." He communicated his displeasure to Elliot. "You have treated my instructions as if they were waste paper which you might treat with entire disregard," he wrote, "and that you were at full liberty to deal with the interests of your country according to your own fancy."[5] Elliot was abruptly recalled, and Sir Henry Pottinger was dispatched to wring out of the intractable Chinese a more promising site for a British base.

When Pottinger arrived he resumed hostilities with the Chinese, sailing his ships up the Yangtze River and menacing Nanking. The new government in Britain opposed the retaining of Hong Kong, but upon sizing up the situation for himself Pottinger too crossed his orders. "This settlement has already advanced too far to admit of its being restored to the authority of the Emperor consistently with the honour . . . of Her Majesty's Crown."[6] On August 29, 1842, he ended the First Opium War with the Treaty of Nanking, in which he secured Hong Kong island for Britain as well as opening five Chinese ports to trade. This treaty was supplemented by a commercial accord, the Treaty of the Bogue, the following year, under which the Chinese were permitted free access to Hong Kong.

"Unequal Treaties"

These agreements were the first of what Chinese history regards as the "unequal treaties," those forced on them by the West. In Chinese eyes this was the nadir of the Celestial Kingdom, when it was carved up by foreign powers. Those who negotiated these treaties are regarded as people who sold

China's territorial integrity for a few pieces of silver. This history explains why the Chinese have always viewed Britain as the imperial power par excellence. It is no coincidence that in the wake of the massacre at Tiananmen Square the Communists have reemphasized the history of the Opium Wars, as a means of countering foreign influences today.

In June 1842 the Treaty of Nanking was ratified by Parliament, and Hong Kong officially became a crown colony. It grew rapidly. With the exception of the site of St. John's Anglican Cathedral, all land was owned by the Crown and leased out. The first leases were for 999 years, others for 99 years; gradually the terms grew less, a fact that would take on great significance in the years leading up to the 1984 Sino-British agreement returning Hong Kong to China. Businesses quickly snapped up the waterfront property and built huge warehouses, and the government tried its best to deal with the lawlessness and piracy that plagued the new settlement. Disease was also a problem, in part because European dress and personal hygiene were ill suited for the tropical clime. In March 1859 the *London Times* summed up home opinion about the colony by noting that Hong Kong "is always connected with some fatal pestilence, some doubtful war, or some discreditable internal struggle."

Nevertheless, the colony continued to grow, for one reason: it was useful. It was useful to the British as a base for their operations in the Pacific and as a free port; and it was useful to the Chinese, who profited handsomely from the riches Hong Kong trade generated. This arrangement of convenience has characterized Hong Kong for most of its century and a half of existence. Indeed, what marked out Hong Kong from the rest of Her Majesty's possessions is that it was from the first a commercial colony, having more to do with the wants and needs of British merchants than with those of British politicians.

But Hong Kong's prosperity has ever been accompanied by

Eastern turbulence. The Second Opium War began in 1856, just as the colony was getting off the ground, largely as a result of disputes over the terms of the previous treaties. Actually, Palmerston had been spoiling for a fight with the truculent Chinese, and they gave him his excuse when they boarded a Hong Kong–registered ship that (though owned by a Chinese) was commanded by a British captain and was flying a British flag. China's refusal to back down soon had the Royal Navy paying another visit to China. This time it had the assistance of French troops, purportedly seeking redress for the murder of a French priest whose body was said to have been chopped up into tiny pieces.

The fighting dragged on for about two years. By May 1860 the advantage had again fallen to the British and their French allies. On October 24, 1860, the British and French marched into the Chinese capital and negotiated the Convention of Peking. The British commander, the Earl of Elgin (son of the purchaser of the famous marbles), allowed his troops to sack the Emperor's Summer Palace—a stunning baroque villa designed by Italian Jesuits—in retribution for the mistreatment of British soldiers.

China's loss was Hong Kong's gain. The Convention of Peking added to Hong Kong's territory the lower part of the Kowloon Peninsula on the mainland, a sliver of land that, though only about 3.5 square miles in area, occupies a strategic position and gave the British secure control over Hong Kong. The limits of the acquisition can still be seen today by anyone who ventures out to Boundary Street.

Thus far all the land the British had extracted from the Chinese had been ceded in perpetuity. But in 1898 this changed with the acquisition of yet more land. Hong Kong had grown all too fast, and by the turn of the century its population of 198,000 was feeling pinched. The weakness of the hated Manchu regime on the mainland meant China was in no position to bargain, and the French, Americans, Russians, Japanese, and Germans had all snatched parts of China for themselves. The British decided to expand their own holdings. What they got was a lease on the New Territories, a mountainous mainland area adjoining Kowloon Peninsula. In one neat swoop this increased the size of British Hong Kong from 32 to 390 square miles. But this time, in the Second Convention of Peking, the land was not ceded to the British. Instead, in deference to the fashion of the day, they got a ninety-nine-year lease on the New Territories, to expire on June 30, 1997.

China was, as always, divided internally, and helpless to defend its territory against grasping foreign powers. Adding insult to injury, foreigners lived in their own little enclaves with their own rules and courts, exempt from Chinese law and authority. Such privileges have irked all Chinese nationalists, Communists no less than others, and the age-old grievances still fester just below the surface. They will do so until that day in 1997 when the last and most irritating foreign flag no longer flies over Chinese soil.

"Pluck and Enterprise"

In the meantime there is money to be made, a happy tradition from the first in Hong Kong. After its founding the settlement quickly acquired all the trappings of a proper colony, with an exclusive Hong Kong Club, a downtown cricket pitch, a proper cathedral, and religious schools to educate the local heathen. A certain smugness developed, as witness an 1893 handbook published locally by the firm of Kelly and Walsh:

> No apology can be necessary for offering a Hand-book to the British Crown Colony of Hongkong. For ages prior to the year 1841, it existed only as a plutonic island of uninviting sterility, apparently capable only of supporting the lowest forms of organisms. To-day, it stands forth before

the world with its City of Victoria and a permanent population of over two hundred thousand souls—a noble monument to British pluck and enterprise.

From its position on the south-eastern shores of the continent of Asia and the great Chinese Empire, to which it originally belonged—and to which it is still supposed to belong by the thousands of Chinese who daily throng the native portions of the City—its roads and buildings constructed at enormous cost, owing to the steep and rocky nature of the ground; the variety of its inhabitants from all the quarters of the globe; its magnificent land-locked harbour, and its reliance for its very existence upon the shipping which is continually entering the harbour from the principal countries and ports of the world—Hongkong is of surpassing interest as a British possession, and its influence upon the future of the neighboring Empire, it is difficult, if not impossible to foretell.

No stranger, however unsympathetic, can pass along the roads and streets of Hongkong without a feeling of wonder and admiration at the almost magical influence, which in so few years, could transform the barren granite mountain sides of the island of Hongkong into one of the most pleasant cities of the earth.

The sentiment was by no means confined to jingoistic Englishmen. Dr. Sun Yat-sen, founder of the Chinese republic and a former medical student in the colony, delivered himself of a similar paean in a commencement address at the University of Hong Kong in 1923. Despite having been banished from Hong Kong in his younger days for "engaging in plots and dangerous conspiracies" against the authorities in neighboring Canton, he did not stint his praises of the crown colony. "Where did I get my revolutionary and modern ideas from?" he asked the students rhetorically.

I got them in the colony of Hong Kong. I compared Heungshan with Hong Kong and, although they are only fifty miles apart the difference of the government impressed me very much. Afterwards I saw the outside world and began to wonder how it was that foreigners, the Englishmen, could do so much as they had done for example with the barren rock of Hong Kong within seventy or eighty years, while in 4,000 years China had no place like Hong Kong.

Dr. Sun exhorted the students to "carry this English example of good government to every part of China."

They never got the chance. True enough, the opium trade was ended at the outset of the century, and the Manchu dynasty finally fell in 1911, replaced by Dr. Sun's Nationalist government. But the new republic was fractured and divided from birth and never really managed to unite the nation, much less make it prosper.

In 1925 Sun died and was succeeded by Chiang Kai-shek, who again set about unifying China. Among the demands of the new government were equality with other world powers, the end of extraterritoriality, of foreign settlements, and of the foreign control of Chinese concessions, and, of course, abrogation of the unequal treaties. The Nationalist ferment seeped into Hong Kong, taking its most spectacular form in the very damaging general strike and boycott of 1925–26.

Hong Kong lasted out the strike as it had lasted out so many other political crises brought about by its neighbor, but soon it was faced with an even more severe menace: Japan. Indeed, only the growing militarism of Japan had distracted Chiang from Hong Kong. The end was to come swiftly in December 1941 as an ill-prepared Hong Kong, with only a few thousand armed men, held out against overwhelming forces until Christmas Day. Churchill had known there was no hope; the Hong Kong navy had only two old destroyers and a few torpedo boats, and the air force four Wildebeest torpedo bombers with no torpedoes and three supermarine Walrus amphibians with no radar. Nonetheless, in his last cabled message to the governor he urged resistance. "The enemy should be compelled to expend the utmost life and equipment," he said. "Every day that you are able to maintain your resistance you and your men can win the lasting honour which we are sure will be your due." Hong Kong's reaction was recorded in his memoirs after the war. "The orders were obeyed in spirit and to the letter and the Hong Kong garrison had fought to the end a good fight, they won indeed the lasting honour."

The attack on Hong Kong came just hours after the Japanese aircraft had bombed Pearl Harbor. Yet it was to take the invaders seventeen days to conquer the territory, a testament to the dedicated resistance of hopelessly outmanned and out-gunned army and reserves. The governor, Sir Mark Young, surrendered on Christmas Day.

The four years of occupation that followed were brutal. British civilians were placed in concentration camps in Stanley on the southern coast, and the Japanese began deporting others. By the time H.M.S. *Redoubtable* steamed back into Hong Kong waters five years later, the colony was in tatters, its harbor choked with the wreckage of destroyed ships, its population reduced by more than a million, and its trade ground to a halt. There was some talk among the Americans about handing over liberated Hong Kong to Chiang—now one of the Five Powers—but the notion was foiled when a freed British internee named Franklin Gimson ran up the Union Jack and reclaimed the territory for Her Majesty im-mediatcly after his release from Stanley prison camp. Once again Hong Kong survived.

The question was, for how long. Barely having recovered from the war, Hong Kong found itself newly imperiled by the rise of the hammer and sickle across the border. In September 1949 the Chinese Communist armies swept southward, com-ing within 100 miles of Hong Kong, and in Peking on October 1 a triumphant Mao Zedong stood at the Gate of Heavenly Peace to proclaim the birth of the People's Republic of China. The red flag was raised to cheers. "Our country will never again be an insulted nation," promised Mao. "The Chinese people have stood up." Hong Kong watched in fascinated horror, and with good reason: the rise of Communism next door would pose its greatest challenge.

"A Problem of People"

When Captain Charles Elliot first secured the island, the British had not imagined it as a home for more than a token number of Chinese. But the Chinese had flocked here from the start. Less than ten years after the British first raised the standard, the colony's Chinese population had gone from under 4,000 to 33,000. It reached 94,000 by 1860, 124,000 by 1870, and 263,000 by the turn of the century. Just before World War II the population topped off at 1.6 million, and though it dropped precipitously during the Japanese occupation it was back up to about 2 million in 1950. Ten years and a million refugees later, it had reached 3 million, and the 1990 figure was 5.8 million. At all stages almost all of the population has been ethnic Chinese; the proportion of expatriates has been very small.

As the numbers illustrate, Hong Kong's population traditionally rises in proportion to turmoil on the mainland. The Taiping and Boxer rebellions, the invading Japanese, and the plundering warlords all created refugees, including even Communists such as Chou En-lai fleeing the wrath of Chiang. But there has never been anything to match the scale of the 1950s, when the Communist victory on the mainland resulted in floods of people with little more than the shirts on their backs. They came by plane, train, and boat—some even swam through shark-infested waters—but mostly they arrived on foot, and they lived anywhere they could: in the streets, under trees, on the hills, in homes that were little more than a few sorry square feet of old boards and tin.

The 1957 Annual Report put out by the Hong Kong government set forth the grim facts in its first chapter, entitled "A Problem of People":

Virtually every sizable vacant site which was not under some form of physical or continuing protection was occupied, and when there was no flat land remaining they moved up to the hillsides and colonized the ravines and slopes which were too steep for normal development. The huts were constructed of such material as they could lay hands on at little or no cost—flattened sheets of tin, wooden boarding, cardboard, sacking slung on frames—every variety of two dimensional material that was light enough to carry and cheap enough to beg or steal or buy for a few dollars. Land was scarce even for the squatters, and the huts were packed like dense honeycombs or irregular warrens at different levels, with little ventilation or light and no regular access.

The shacks themselves were crowded beyond endurance. In some cases five or six human beings existed in a cubicle measuring 40 square feet. Density was at a rate of 2,000 persons to an acre in single story huts. There was, of course, no sanitation, and there was seldom any organized system of refuse disposal. There was in most cases no mains water immediately available, and water for all purposes had to be carried long distances from communal standpipes or collected from such hillside streams as the season allowed. Cooking fuel was charcoal or wood used in open "chatties" (small cooking stoves), and at night some of the huts were lit with kerosene lamps or candles. Chickens, ducks, and pigs shared the huts or the narrow congested areas around them. . . .

In such conditions every kind of vice flourished. Drugs were manufactured, sold, and stored; there were divans, brothels, and gambling houses; every form of crime was sheltered by the anonymity of these dark places.[7]

On top of this came tragedy. On Christmas Day 1953, a fire in the Shek Kip Mei squatter area left 50,000 people homeless in a single night.

The United Nations High Commissioner for Refugees advised that Hong Kong couldn't possible retain all those refugees from China, and the generally accepted view was that Hong Kong's peak capacity was somewhere in the neighborhood of 1.2 million. But not only did Hong Kong survive—it bloomed. It did so, moreover, in spite of the severe blow dealt by the Korean War, when a U.N. embargo on China trade caused Hong Kong to lose its largest trading partner overnight. The colony continued to prosper, in large part because of the skills, experience, and spirit of the refugees from China. "They were the reason Hong Kong flourished so," says actress Nancy Kwan, who actually grew up in the Hong Kong of Suzie Wong. "The people who built up Hong Kong were the same people who fled from the Communists in the 1950s. They settled in Hong Kong because . . . they literally couldn't go any farther." So they set about recasting Hong Kong in the dynamic image of pre-Communist Shanghai.

Three years after the publication of "A Problem of People," the Hong Kong government, to its credit, officially reversed itself. Its 1960 Annual Report put it this way:

> The new arrivals whose presence created so many of Hong Kong's difficulties have also, many of them, materially assisted in that successful change-over to an industrial economy which has provided the general prosperity without which a policy of integration would not have been possible. Many of these new arrivals brought with them capital, industrial skill, technical efficiency, and in some cases even industrial plant; and these combined with the resilience and resource of the existing population, laid the foundation for a rapidly developing industrialization.[8]

Hong Kong has prospered ever since, albeit at times with an uneasy eye over its shoulder at its Communist neighbor. In 1966, in the midst of the Cultural Revolution, Red Guards moved into the Portuguese colony of Macau, just thirty-eight miles away, bringing the government there to the point of capitulation. The next summer Hong Kong itself was the scene of almost daily incidents of violence. Provocateurs incited riots, and Government House was covered with Chinese characters calling for death for the "blond-haired, blue-eyed foreign devils." Mobs chanted and screamed, holding aloft their little red books of Chairman Mao's sayings. There were bombs concealed in paper bags, bombs that looked like little toys, bombs stuffed in bottles. Only the coolness of the government, and the unprecedented courage of the police force (the ethnic Chinese in particular), prevented the Cultural Revolution from finishing off the colony.

Once again, Hong Kong survived. But survival this time bred a dangerous arrogance, the feeling that Hong Kong could survive *anything*. It had withstood Communist and Nationalist revolutions on the mainland, a savage Japanese occupation, and Red Guard–provoked riots in front of the governor's residence to become by the late 1970s one of the most attractive investments in all Asia, and if 1997 was a question mark, well, they would deal with that when they came to it. The optimism only escalated when Mao died and the Gang of Four was removed from power, leaving Deng Xiaoping in control. Deng was too cagey, too "pragmatic" to ruin a good thing, thought the optimists. After all, Mao himself had allowed Hong Kong to continue because he found it useful, even after Khrushchev had taunted him about the "stinking rose" of colonialism on his doorstep. There was even talk of Hong Kong's "ruling China."

It was to prove a dangerous conceit.

2

The Joint Declaration

O N SEPTEMBER 23, 1982, Margaret Thatcher emerged from talks with Chinese Premier Zhao Ziyang and stepped into the grey Peking day. As she left the Great Hall of the People, she stumbled and fell on her hands and knees. To the superstitious Cantonese it was a bad omen. "She has decided to kowtow to Chairman Mao at last," said some.

In fact Britain's prime minister had taken a tough line over Hong Kong. The actual details of her meetings with Zhao and paramount leader Deng Xiaoping have never been made public; what is known is that the Chinese were greatly put out by her forthrightness. Fresh from her victory in the Falklands, she was not in a conciliatory mood. Probably she repeated Britain's determination to retain a presence in Hong Kong after 1997. Almost certainly she insisted on the validity of the aforementioned "unequal treaties," an affront to any nationalist government and especially to a Communist one.

At the press conference in Peking, Mrs. Thatcher read from the bland joint statement that the two sides had agreed upon:

> The two leaders of the two countries held far-reaching talks in a friendly atmosphere on the future of Hong Kong. Both leaders made clear their respective positions on the subject. They agreed to enter talks through diplomatic channels following the visit, with the common aim of maintaining the stability and prosperity of Hong Kong.[1]

What the Iron Lady did not know was that she had been set up by her hosts. In a deliberate breach of protocol, the Chinese had released a statement through the New China News Agency whose gist was that China intended to resume sovereignty over Hong Kong (Hong Kong island, Kowloon, and the New Territories) at an appropriate time to be determined by the PRC itself. An Italian reporter asked her about this Chinese declaration, but she declined comment, noting that it would be premature to remark on something she had not yet read.

Unruffled by the diplomatic slap in the face, Mrs. Thatcher flew on to Shanghai and Canton before arriving in Hong Kong a few days later. On September 27 she called another press conference, in which she revealed some of the details of the talks in Peking and said she was confident the two nations would "reconcile their differences" over Hong Kong. This time she noted that Britain sought to renegotiate the lease on the New Territories, whose forthcoming expiry on June 30, 1997, was of course the impetus for the Sino-British discussions. The so-called unequal treaties, she insisted, were legal and valid under international law.

Then she administered a slap of her own. "Those who do not honor one treaty," she said, "will not honor another."

The statement was not intended to please Peking, and it did not. The offense was aggravated, moreover, by her further talk about Britain's "moral responsibility" to the people of Hong Kong. Routine perhaps to Western ears, such talk was guaranteed to infuriate the Chinese, who had historically maintained they were the only representatives of the colony's ethnic Chinese population. The next day, Mrs. Thatcher left.

Peking's response was swift and unequivocal. In a September 30 editorial, the New China News Agency laid out the PRC's position. The unequal treaties, it said, were "illegal, and therefore null and void." The Communist Chinese government intended to pursue its "sacred mission" of recovering

Hong Kong and righting the wrong done by British imperialists more than a century earlier.

The Hong Kong dollar, already shaky, did not respond well to the Thatcher visit.

Many accounts of these critical days have blamed Mrs. Thatcher for playing her hand badly in Peking and thereby wiping out any chance there might have been of keeping Hong Kong under British control. The damage was reinforced by her suggestions that China couldn't be trusted to keep its word.[2] Had she been a tad more politic, the feeling goes, the Chinese might not have been provoked into saying they were determined to take Hong Kong back whatever the cost. At the very least she ought to have known what a sore spot the unequal treaties were.

In fairness to Mrs. Thatcher, however, it must be said that Hong Kong's fate had largely been sealed in 1979, when then governor Sir Murray MacLehose visited Peking. A tall, aristocratic Scotsman, MacLehose had been a career officer in Her Majesty's diplomatic corps and was ambassador to South Vietnam during the Tet Offensive. In the late 1950s and early 1960s he had served as political advisor to the Hong Kong government and therefore as the link between Hong Kong and Britain in matters that concerned Peking. When he became governor in 1971, MacLehose inherited a Hong Kong that had recovered from the violent riots of 1967, when the Cultural Revolution had spilled over into the territory. Popular with the Cantonese, he served as governor until 1982.

Sir Murray's meeting with Deng Xiaoping in 1979 marked the first time that a governor of Hong Kong had paid an official visit to Peking. No joint statement was issued after the meeting. But at an April 6 press conference, the governor said that Chinese leaders had stressed Hong Kong's importance to the development of the mainland. "Vice Premier Deng Xiaoping formally requested me to ask investors in Hong Kong to put their hearts at ease," Sir Murray told reporters.

What he didn't say—and what started Hong Kong down the disastrous path it now finds itself on—was that he had unwisely pressed for more than Deng's offer of a gentlemen's agreement. What he wanted was a written guarantee, the effect of which, at least in Chinese eyes, would be a brand-new unequal treaty. The Chinese quietly told him to drop it, and in Peking they complained privately that Britain was "trying to force our hand."

But Britain pressed on. The reason was, ironically, the business community. As the 1997 expiry of the New Territories lease from China approached, real estate operators and banks (particularly foreign-held ones) wanted written assurance before they approved any mortgages in the New Territories (which include more than 90 per cent of the land area of today's Hong Kong) that extended beyond the fateful day. They wanted a legal document, signed, sealed, and delivered.

Peking's Dilemma

That demand is grandfather to today's exodus. In a remarkably prescient article in the *South China Morning Post* in 1978, Professor T. L. Tsim of Shaw College pointed out that the British were pushing Hong Kong toward rocky shoals:

> [The business community] want to know from the Chinese government what assurances they have that their investments will be safe so that they can carry on making the kind of profit they have been making for the last thirty years.
>
> The answer is none. There is no assurance and there will be no assurance. Anyone who understands the Chinese Government will know that no explicit affirmation or guarantee will be forthcoming. The Government in Peking has never recognized the unequal treaties. It has said time and again that Hong Kong is Chinese soil. The British administration is here only on sufferance.
>
> It may be in China's interest to maintain the status quo in Hong Kong, but, having made known its position [on

unequal treaties] in such definite, unequivocal terms, Peking could not now extend a lease which was imposed on China through an unequal treaty without compromising its authority in the eyes of its people.

The strong man syndrome of Chinese politics dictates that the Government must not only be strong but must be seen to be strong. China cannot—therefore will not—formally extend the lease of the New Territories.

The most it will say about the future of Hong Kong is that this question will be resolved after the problem of Taiwan has been disposed of. This is a convenient ploy, and a positive one. Investors and bankers must take it from there. They must be content to read the signs as best they can.[3]

In short, the key thing was not to force Peking into taking a stand; not reacting would constitute a tacit endorsement of the status quo. As for the banks' problem, the way around it would have been to have the (Communist) Bank of China take the lead in extending mortgages in the New Territories beyond 1997, thus giving the kind of implicit recognition of the status quo that China has given in a host of other areas. Unlike the legalistic Anglo-Saxon, the Chinese mind has no problem finding ways to accommodate apparent contradictions.

Dr. Peter Wesley-Smith, senior lecturer in law at the University of Hong Kong, has pointed out that China regards the 1898 convention by which Britain leased the New Territories as "an unequal treaty, of no legal effect, thus incapable of expiring and . . . irrelevant."[4] The long and short of it was that Peking could hardly demand the return of Hong Kong on the basis of a treaty whose validity it has never recognized.

Such signs as there were, moreover, suggested that the Chinese were reluctant to give up the existing arrangement, which they found most useful. In 1977, one year after the Gang of Four was finally deposed, Party Chairman Hua Guo-feng spelled out the mainland's intentions toward Hong Kong in a "Report on the World Situation" to the Communist Party of China. The report argued against altering the status quo for the time being: the recovery of both Hong Kong and Macau should not even be mentioned for the "next ten or twenty years or even a considerably longer time so that Hong Kong and Macau may enjoy a period of relative stability for development." Noting the improved relations with London on the issue, Hua put Hong Kong in the perspective of more pressing Chinese goals. "Some advocate that we proceed with the recovery of Hong Kong after liberation of Taiwan," he told party leaders. "Although we have not expressed it publicly, the possibility cannot be entirely ruled out."[5] The operative word was *publicly*. That was about as clear an indication as Peking ever provides.

As late as 1981 the Chinese would still have preferred to let the matter of Hong Kong drop. But the British, prodded by the business community, kept pushing. Partly this was because they had calculated that the rise of Deng Xiaoping (upon whom one of the greatest of journalistic accolades, "pragmatist," has long been bestowed) and the concomitant dulling of Maoism opened up new horizons for Sino-British cooperation; the idea was that the mainland's determination to modernize put Hong Kong in its best position ever to renegotiate its future. Some raised the possibility of retaining British administration under Chinese sovereignty, a nice idea on paper but one never taken seriously by the mainland. The sandy foundation upon which all these optimistic assumptions rested was that economic imperatives could override the goals of politics, Chinese Communist politics in particular.

A Foreordained Outcome

This was bound to result in disaster, because once Britain decided it could not do without another agreement from the PRC, mainland rule over Hong Kong was more or less inevitable. So obvious is this in hindsight that some observers think Britain had decided to abandon Hong Kong long before the talks. The opinion was lent some credence by former prime minister Edward Heath's admission that he knew of such plans as far back as 1971. Under this theory, Britain was to take a blustery line at the outset precisely to provoke the Chinese into insisting on taking back the colony.

Whatever the truth of British intentions, the outcome was foreordained once official talks began, which means that Mrs. Thatcher's controversial 1982 visit did not so much precipitate the Chinese reaction as make it explicit. Granted, she got Chinese backs up by standing firm on the unequal treaties and by talking about Britain's responsibilities to Hong Kong. But there wasn't much else on which to rest her case. The lease on the New Territories was indeed due to expire, and a Falklands-style war with the PRC was out of the question. All Britain could hope to do was to persuade Peking that a prosperous Hong Kong was in the PRC's interests and to convince the people of Hong Kong that Peking understood this. Although historians will long dispute the exact effect her visit had on the negotiations that followed, once it came down to a deal, any deal, the interests of Hong Kong were destined to come up short.

The Chinese understood this implicitly. In the wake of Mrs. Thatcher's visit they launched an all-out propaganda offensive against her, directed especially at her notions of Britain's relationship with the Hong Kongers themselves. It was classic united-front agitprop, calculated to appeal to the latent Chinese nationalism of the Hong Kong public.

This was the background of the secret talks that began almost immediately after Mrs. Thatcher's departure from Hong Kong in October 1982. The British were represented by their ambassador to China, Sir Percy Craddock; the only participant from Hong Kong was Robin McLaren, the governor's political advisor. The main purpose at this point was to set an agenda and establish a procedure.

The next round came the following summer, and this time the governor, Sir Edward Youde, traveled to Peking to participate. At a press conference before his departure, a reporter pressed him to say whom he would represent at the talks. "I am the governor of Hong Kong," Sir Edward replied. "Whom else would I represent?" This was something of a *faux pas*, inasmuch as the Chinese had all along insisted that they, not the British, who were there illegally, represented the people and interests of Hong Kong. They contended that the governor was there solely as a representative of the British, and in the pro-PRC press he was pilloried for his remark. That might have been expected; the damning thing was that the Foreign Office never backed Sir Edward up and thereby acknowledged China's claim by default.

Had Britain identified its interests with those of Hong Kong, things might have worked out differently. But the row over Sir Edward's status illustrated one of the key weaknesses of the whole negotiation process, a weakness that continues to mar handling of the 1997 question today: the people of Hong Kong have had no say in the shape of their future. Unfortunately, this arrangement continues to serve both London and Peking exceptionally well.

To ensure that their position was taken, the Chinese emphasized their opposition to Hong Kong participation in the second round of talks by refusing to grant an entry visa to the head of the Hong Kong Government Information Services, Peter Tsao, a Hong Kong–born citizen who carries a full British passport. The aim was to nip any attempt to give Hong Kong a say and, worse, a potential veto. Peking repeated its view that 1997 was a bilateral matter between Britain and China and that the people of Hong Kong were already represented adequately by the Chinese government. The opinion of Hong Kongers themselves—most of whom are either refugees from the PRC or the children of such refugees—was never known. Nor was it ever solicited. In a pattern that would be repeated with tragic frequency over the coming few years, Britain's acquiescence both weakened its own position and, more critically, thwarted the emergence of any real Hong Kong voice.

"One Country, Two Systems"

Even without such a voice, the evidently irreconcilable positions taken by London and Peking ensured little progress in the talks. As each side looked for a way around the impasse, Deng began to float the idea of "one country, two systems." Ostensibly this was a formula designed to permit Taiwan, Macau, and Hong Kong to reunite with the mainland without giving up their capitalist economic systems; the PRC, it was hinted, had even amended its own constitution just to accommodate such a union. Another, related phrase began to be heard as well—"Hong Kong people ruling Hong Kong." This was Peking's way of assuring a nervous Hong Kong that the PRC would not be sending cadres down from other parts of China to govern the colony once it resumed control.

The secrecy surrounding the talks fed wild rumors nonetheless, and the Hong Kong dollar and stock markets did not take it well. Businessmen, jittery over the fuzziness of the future, were not reassured by a host of Chinese statements from PRC officials, party organizers, or pro-mainland papers inside Hong Kong echoing the PRC line. On September 5, 1983, for example, a story from the New China News Agency quoted scores of Hong Kong trade unions to the effect that the colony ought to be reunited with the motherland. "Separation of these would prolong British colonial control of Hong Kong, intolerable to the Chinese people, including the Hong Kong workers," said the news agency.[6] In an interview in the *Financial Times*, the Foreign Ministry's Zhou Nan (later to head the Chinese negotiating team) said that "sovereignty and administration are inseparable."[7] In Peking the *People's Daily* savaged Britain for "seeking vainly to act as representatives of Hong Kong's residents using the so-called Hong Kong 'popular feeling' to apply pressure on the Chinese government to attain their goal of obstructing China from recovering its territory and sovereignty."[8]

In short, China was making it clear that there could be no British role after 1997. The Hong Kong dollar slid to a historic low against the U.S. dollar, and the stock market fell by 64 points to 785. To this day some observers speculate that the British deliberately allowed the market to take a dive as a means of pressuring the PRC into coming around.

If so, it didn't work. China continued the propaganda offensive. PRC officials produced a film called *The Burning of the Summer Palace*, an account of the Anglo-French expeditionary force that in 1860 looted and torched the Jesuit-designed palace of the emperor; the obvious intention was to arouse Hong Kongers' latent Chinese nationalism. China stepped up its war of words, too. In Peking, former foreign minister Ji Pengfei, then head of the Hong Kong and Macau Affairs office, called those who said Hong Kongers were not in favor of reunification "liars." Ji further announced that China would issue a unilateral statement on Hong Kong's future if the talks had not produced an agreement by September 1984. Now there was a deadline.

The Thaw

By the fifth round of talks in mid-October 1983, there had finally been a thaw. Although the reason has never been given, the British ambassador to Peking had delivered a letter from Mrs. Thatcher that, in marked contrast to the John Bull tone she had struck earlier, more or less accepted the Chinese position. Sources say she modified her stand on the validity of the unequal treaties and on the continued British presence after 1997. Whatever the content, the new atmosphere was reflected in a statement by both sides after the talks saying they had been "useful and constructive." By giving up the insistence on sovereignty, Britain had given new life to the talks. It marked the turning point in Hong Kong's future.

In debate in Commons, Robert Adley, chairman of the British-Chinese parliamentary group, insisted it was imperative "to keep the details of the negotiations secret." The minister of state in charge of Hong Kong, Richard Luce, echoed Adley's calls for secrecy and added that the negotiations were being conducted against the backdrop of increasing joint ventures between Britain and the PRC[9]—an interesting aside in light of charges by some critics that Britain sold out Hong Kong for commercial gain in the form of lucrative contracts inside China.

Now that Britain had dropped the insistence on sovereignty, the talks took on a more relaxed air. What were left to settle now were the details of the impending transfer of power. Ji Penfei told a group of visitors from the New Territories (official PRC positions were frequently made known through talks with a selected group of visitors) that Hong Kong would be able to keep things pretty much the way they were for at least fifty years after 1997. He said that guarantees of the liberties the people of Hong Kong enjoyed would be written into a Basic Law, or mini-constitution, to govern the territory after it had returned to the Chinese fold. As 1983 came to a close, Britain and China were moving close to an agreement. In their otherwise cryptic statement, the word "progress" was inserted for the first time.

Drafting the Agreement

In January 1984, the English-language *China Daily*, a PRC house organ, published an interview with Ji that remarkably foreshadowed the terms of the final agreement. Hong Kong, he said, would enjoy "a high degree of autonomy." The British legal system, purged of its colonial character, would remain basically in force. Government officials would be drawn from the local population, and Hong Kong would have the right to enter into separate agreements with foreign powers on matters not relating to foreign policy or security. It would naturally continue to be a free port.

A month later, there was a bit of flurry when Roger Lobo, the senior unofficial member of Hong Kong's Legislative Council, announced that the council planned to debate the whole question of 1997 before Britain and China came to any agreement. To those not familiar with Hong Kong (and even to many who are), the role of the colony's Legislative Council seems horribly complicated. Its members sit on it by virtue of either their position in government (e.g., the chief secretary), an appointment from the governor, or an election by a functional constituency (e.g., doctors, lawyers, labor); in September 1991 the mix was further complicated when eighteen of the sixty seats were opened to direct election by the people. The Executive Council, by contrast, functions as a cabinet. But the governor presides over both councils, and in practice they are without teeth. Indeed, not until Martin Lee introduced an anti-gerrymander bill in January 1991 had a member ever introduced a bill not put forth by the government.

Even so, China objected vigorously even to the idea that a Hong Kong body would debate the Joint Declaration, and the united front moved quickly to condemn the move. In the end the debate was relatively innocuous, and the negotiations went on much as they had before, almost as though the Legislative Council debate hadn't mattered.

It hadn't.

That same summer (1984) the Hong Kong government started up a new working group to begin the "shadow talks" accompanying the formal negotiations. These side talks dealt with some of the technical details and would hardly be worth mentioning, save that the team was led by David Wilson, a member of the Foreign Office who years before had taken some time out from his diplomatic career to edit a scholarly publication on China. In less than three years he would take over as governor after Sir Edward Youde was struck down by a heart attack in Peking.

China was also becoming more candid. On June 22, Deng had two meetings with visitors from Hong Kong: one with a group of prominent businessmen, the other with Sir S. Y. Chung, Lydia Dunn, and Q. W. Lee, all unofficial members of the Legislative and Executive councils in Hong Kong. To the businessmen, Deng repeated the assurance that Hong Kong would remain unchanged for fifty years after 1997. But his attitude toward the council members was telling. He said to them that the question of Hong Kong would be resolved bilaterally between Britain and China, thus putting to rest any talk of a "three-legged stool." Deng even went so far as to tell them that they "should make use of this chance to understand more about Peking, the People's Republic of China, and our Chinese people, as it will be very useful to you."[10] The implied disparagement of their political service in Hong Kong was reinforced by the New China News Agency's references to the members as simply "residents of Hong Kong" and by the *South China Morning Post* story headlined "Humiliation." The message sent to Hong Kong Chinese was, Peking Knows Best.

Deng also included a shocker, one that has taken on even more ominous tones today. Contrary to earlier assurances from Peking, he stated flatly that People's Liberation Army contingents would indeed be stationed in Hong Kong after 1997. Earlier promises, he told Hong Kong reporters, were simply "bullshit." "Now go print it," he dared them.[11] The Hang Seng index took a nosedive.

At the end of July, Mrs. Thatcher sent her foreign secretary, Sir Geoffrey Howe, to Peking to work out the final differences with Premier Zhao. As Sir Geoffrey was leaving, Deng thanked him profusely for what he and Mrs. Thatcher had done. The head of the Chinese negotiating team, Zhou Nan, was even lyrical, quoting from a Sung Dynasty poem: "Just as the weary traveler despairs of finding a road, lo, a village appears and the shade of willows and riotous flowers beckons."[12] Sir Geoffrey preferred sturdy Saxon prose. "I am glad to say that very substantial progress has been made," he said. "We have agreed: first, the framework and key clauses of an agreement which will preserve Hong Kong's unique economic system and way of life; secondly, that this agreement and its annexes will all be legally binding; thirdly, satisfactory provisions for liaison and consultation after conclusion of the agreement."[13]

In what in retrospect is a most ironic note, the foreign secretary took pains to insist that in the run-up to 1997 the Crown would not become a lame duck. The British and Chinese governments firmly agreed, he said, that "the British Government will remain responsible for the administration of Hong Kong until 1997. Let there be no doubt that we shall fulfill that responsibility up to the date."[14]

Now it was only a matter of the fine print. By September 18, the British and Chinese sides had finalized all but a few points, and on September 26, 1984, the agreement was initialed, in time for China's National Day, October 1.

The Joint Declaration

Almost immediately a British White Paper on "The Draft Agreement Between the Government of the United Kingdom of Great Britain and Northern Ireland and the Government of the People's Republic of China on the Future of Hong Kong" was released to a Hong Kong public that had remained in the dark for two years. Crowds snapped up every available copy.

It was a remarkable document, mapping out the transfer of sovereignty over a thriving capitalist enclave from an indifferent European democracy to an aggressive Asian despotism.

The structure was somewhat complex: a relatively brief joint declaration, a long annex describing how post-1997 Hong Kong would be run, and two shorter annexes dealing with technical questions regarding land leases and the establishment of a Joint Liaison Group to implement the agreement in the intervening years. In addition each side added its own memorandum, one of which, the Chinese, included a decidedly pedantic list of explanatory notes.

The gist of the agreement was that although sovereignty over Hong Kong was to move from London to Peking, life in Hong Kong was to remain more or less the same until at least 2047. The Joint Declaration itself is concise and is worth including here in its entirety, so that the reader can understand the enthusiasm that its release occasioned:

> The Government of the United Kingdom of Great Britain and Northern Ireland and the Government of the People's Republic of China have reviewed with satisfaction the friendly relations existing between the two Governments and peoples in recent years and agreed that a proper negotiated settlement of the question of Hong Kong, which is left over from the past, is conducive to the maintenance of the prosperity and stability of Hong Kong and to the further strengthening and development of the relations between the two countries on a new basis. To this end, they have, after talks between the delegations of the two Governments, agreed to declare as follows:
>
> 1. The Government of the People's Republic of China declares that to recover the Hong Kong area (including Hong Kong Island, Kowloon and the New Territories, hereinafter referred to as Hong Kong) is the common aspiration of the entire Chinese people, and that it has decided to resume the exercise of sovereignty over Hong Kong with effect from 1 July 1997.
>
> 2. The Government of the United Kingdom declares that it will restore Hong Kong to the People's Republic of China with effect from 1 July 1997.

3. The Government of the People's Republic of China declares that the basic policies of the People's Republic of China regarding Hong Kong are as follows:

(1) Upholding national unity and territorial integrity and taking account of the history of Hong Kong and its realities, the People's Republic of China has decided to establish, in accordance with the provisions of Article 31 of the Constitution of the People's Republic of China, a Hong Kong Special Administrative Region upon resuming the exercise of sovereignty over Hong Kong.

(2) The Hong Kong Special Administrative Region will be directly under the authority of the Central People's Government of the People's Republic of China. The Hong Kong Special Administrative Region will enjoy a high degree of autonomy, except in foreign and defence affairs which are the responsibilities of the Central People's Government.

(3) The Hong Kong Special Administrative Region will be vested with executive, legislative and independent judicial power, including that of final adjudication. The laws currently in force in Hong Kong will remain basically unchanged.

(4) The Government of the Hong Kong Special Administrative Region will be composed of local inhabitants. The chief executive will be appointed by the Central People's Government on the basis of the results of elections or consultations to be held locally. Principal officials will be nominated by the chief executive of the Hong Kong Special Administrative Region for appointment by the Central People's Government. Chinese and foreign nationals previously working in the public and police services in the government departments of Hong Kong may remain in employment. British and other foreign nationals may also be employed to serve as advisers or hold certain public posts in government departments of the Hong Kong Special Administrative Region.

(5) The current social and economic systems in Hong Kong will remain unchanged, and so will the life-

style. Rights and freedoms, including those of the person, of speech, of the press, of assembly, of association, of travel, of movement, of correspondence, of strike, of choice of occupation, of academic research and of religious belief will be ensured by law in the Hong Kong Special Administrative Region. Private property, ownership of enterprises, legitimate right of inheritance and foreign investment will be protected by law.

(6) The Hong Kong Special Administrative Region will retain the status of a free port and a separate customs territory.

(7) The Hong Kong Special Administrative Region will retain the status of an international financial centre, and its markets for foreign exchange, gold, securities and futures will continue. There will be free flow of capital. The Hong Kong dollar will continue to circulate and remain freely convertible.

(8) The Hong Kong Special Administrative Region will have independent finances. The Central People's Government will not levy taxes on the Hong Kong Special Administrative Region.

(9) The Hong Kong Special Administrative Region may establish mutually beneficial economic relations with the United Kingdom and other countries, whose economic interests in Hong Kong will be given due regard.

(10) Using the name of "Hong Kong, China," the Hong Kong Special Administrative Region may on its own maintain and develop economic and cultural relations and conclude relevant agreements with states, regions and relevant international organisations. The Government of the Hong Kong Special Administrative Region may on its own issue travel documents for entry into and exit from Hong Kong.

(11) The maintenance of public order in the Hong Kong Special Administrative Region will be the responsibility of the Government of the Hong Kong Special Administrative Region.

(12) The above-stated basic policies of the People's

Republic of China regarding Hong Kong and the elaboration of them in Annex I to this Joint Declaration will be stipulated, in a Basic Law of the Hong Kong Special Administrative Region of the People's Republic of China, by the National People's Congress of the People's Republic of China, and they will remain unchanged for 50 years.

4. The Government of the United Kingdom and the Government of the People's Republic of China declare that, during the transitional period between the date of the entry into force of this Joint Declaration and 30 June 1997, the Government of the United Kingdom will be responsible for the administration of Hong Kong with the object of maintaining and preserving its economic prosperity and social stability; and that the Government of the People's Republic of China will give its cooperation in this connection.

5. The Government of the United Kingdom and the Government of the People's Republic of China declare that, in order to ensure a smooth transfer of government in 1997, and with a view to the effective implementation of this Joint Declaration, a Sino-British Joint Liaison Group will be set up when this Joint Declaration enters into force; and that it will be established and will function in accordance with the provisions of Annex II to this Joint Declaration.

6. The Government of the United Kingdom and the Government of the People's Republic of China declare that land leases in Hong Kong and other related matters will be dealt with in accordance with the provisions of Annex III to this Joint Declaration.

7. The Government of the United Kingdom and the Government of the People's Republic of China agree to implement the preceding declarations and the Annexes to this Joint Declaration.

8. This Joint Declaration is subject to ratification and shall enter into force on the date of the exchange of instruments of ratification, which shall take place in Beijing before 30 June 1985. This Joint Declaration and its Annexes shall be equally binding.

The annexes clarified some of these points and added some details. For example, one calls for a Basic Law, to be drafted by China, that would explicitly note that "the socialist system and socialist policy shall not be practiced in the Hong Kong Special Administrative Region and that Hong Kong's previous capitalist system and lifestyle shall remain unchanged for fifty years." Elsewhere it repeats the promises that cadres would not be sent in to run Hong Kong, that instead the government would be "composed of local inhabitants," and that English would be maintained as an official language—of particular importance to the courts, based as they are on common law. The courts themselves were to be independent and "free from any interference."

In lawyerly detail the rest of the document charts such diverse areas as education and customs treaties, all with the intent of assuring people that nothing much was really going to change. Chinese troops would be stationed in Hong Kong, for example, but they "shall not interfere in the internal affairs" of the new Special Administrative Region. On the question of residency, it stipulates that Hong Kong people or those with seven years' residence in the colony would be granted identity cards, and that some non-Chinese nationals with a similar residency would also get identity cards (though not Chinese passports). The Joint Liaison Group would *not* become "an organ of power" and would stick to consultation and exchange of information. And land leases could now be issued that would extend into the period after the transfer of power.

The trickiest matter was nationality. On the British side, successive changes in immigration law beginning in 1962 had stripped Hong Kongers of the right to live in Britain, even though they remain British subjects. The breakdown is as follows: of Hong Kong's population—predominantly ethnic Chinese—of 5.8 million, about 3.25 million hold British passports (but without the right of abode); the rest, with the exception of a tiny expatriate population and a few accidents of empire (e.g., the colony's sizable Indian contingent), are permanent residents who emigrated from China and hold certificates of identity. The PRC's view is that all Hong Kong Chinese without the right of abode in the United Kingdom are Chinese nationals and that the British passports they may carry are simply travel documents. For quite different reasons, Britain found this approach as convenient as China did, and consequently the Joint Declaration stipulates that the carriers of these second-class British passports "will not be entitled to British consular protection in the Hong Kong Special Administrative Region."

The deal was done. In December Mrs. Thatcher again flew to Peking to meet with party leaders. This time everything went smoothly. There were no offensive words about honoring treaties and no falls from the steps of the Great Hall of the People. The week before, the prime minister had entertained a new Soviet leader named Mikhail Gorbachev; there were more pressing things on her mind. Only one evening of her trip was devoted to a Hong Kong whose fate had just been sealed.

On December 21, Mrs. Thatcher held a press conference in Hong Kong. Unlike her meetings in Peking, this one did not come off well. She answered incorrectly about key details and had to be corrected by the governor. She said she had not known "the content of any talks" between Sir Murray Mac-Lehose and the Chinese authorities back in 1979, when the fateful transfer was set in motion. And when she was challenged by reporter Emily Lau about the morality of delivering more than five million people into the hands of a Communist regime, the Iron Lady responded with schoolmarmish dismissal:

What do you think would have happened if we had not attempted to get an agreement? 1997—92 per cent of the territory would automatically have returned to China without reassurances. . . . I think you would have had great cause to complain had the government of Great Britain done nothing until 1997, and I believe that most of the people in Hong Kong think the same. You may be a solitary exception.[15]

A few moments later, the Iron Lady left the Legislative Council chambers, climbed into a waiting car, and left Hong Kong to ponder its fate.

3

The Retreat

Within Hong Kong, initial reaction to the Joint Declaration was enthusiastic. With Deng Xiaoping apparently committed to reform on the mainland and Hong Kong itself already a model Chinese city, there was talk of Hong Kong's taking over the PRC instead of the reverse.

On the day the agreement was signed, the editor of the leading English-language weekly in the region walked into his office with a Union Jack T-shirt and a bottle of champagne and sat down to attack those who had their doubts about the accord. In a column entitled "Dark voices prophesying doom," he focused much of his attack on Bernard Levin, who in his own column in the *Times* of London had likened Foreign Secretary Geoffrey Howe's return from Peking with the finalized treaty to Chamberlain's return from Munich almost a half-century earlier. But the editor was confident that history would not strike twice. "To suppose that Hongkong could be a modern antibiotic now to be reinserted into China, to help accelerate the cure of the Marxist disease and aid recuperation by modernisation, playing a part out of all proportion to its size in putting China back on to its traditional search for peace, stability and prosperity—the Confucian Golden Mean—is no longer a mere opium dream," he wrote.[1] He had seen the future, and it worked.

In Parliament Sir Geoffrey hailed the accord as a "bold and imaginative plan" that "as a means of reconciling the apparently irreconcilable . . . could have implications for problems in other parts of the world."[2] Both of the colony's English-language newspapers, the *South China Morning Post* and the *Hongkong Standard*, chimed in with endorsements. The *Post* called it "a document that, if nothing else, will be read by future generations as a landmark of good sense, human reasonableness, delicate compromise and high idealism."[3] "Meets the wishes of the Hong Kong people," added the most important Chinese-language paper, *Ming Pao*.[4] Michael Sandberg, chairman of the Hongkong and Shanghai Banking Corporation, the de facto central bank for the colony, dismissed fears that China might not be as good as its word by asking, "What guarantees are there that there will be a democratic capitalist market in West Germany in 1997?"[5]

The Legislative Council debated the agreement on October 15–16, and all but two of the forty-seven members endorsed it. Dame Lydia Dunn, then a member of the council, contended that China "would surely not have committed so much negotiating effort into reaching an agreement" if it had "no intention of adhering to the terms of the agreement."[6]

Sir S. Y. Chung, the senior appointed member of the Executive Council, issued a press release endorsing the Joint Declaration on behalf of all the unofficial members of the council: "It is our belief that what we have today is the best agreement possible and one which we, the unofficial members of the Executive Council, can commend to the people of Hong Kong in good conscience. The world at large will observe the good faith with which it is being implemented, and we trust the people of Hong Kong can take heart from this."[7] The Executive Council as a whole gave its approval to the agreement, as did the Urban Council and the eighteen District Boards.

The business community expressed its support also. The chief executive of Hutchinson Whampoa, Simon Murray (now head of a group called Honour Hong Kong), argued that the

Joint Declaration "induces a great sigh of relief as the uncertainties of the last two years are put to rest and we can get on with running our lives and futures again."[8] The president of the Chinese Manufacturers Association, Ngai Shui-kit, concurred. Allen Lee, an appointed member of the Legislative Council, called the concept behind the Joint Declaration "the boldest political thought that contemporary history has ever encountered. . . . I support [it] with clear conscience."[9]

The roll call of applause was a Who's Who of Hong Kong's most important groups. The agreement was endorsed by the Chinese General Chamber of Commerce (composed of more than 3,000 companies), the Chinese Manufacturers' Association, the Federation of Hong Kong Garment Manufacturers, the Federation of Hong Kong Industries, the Hong Kong Factory Owners Association, the Hong Kong General Chamber of Commerce, the American Chamber of Commerce in Hong Kong, and a host of other social and labor organizations from the Federation of Education Workers to the Vegetable Foods and Grocery Hawkers Welfare and Fraternity Association.[10] In fact, virtually *all* Hong Kong organizations and institutions lined up behind the accord.

To be sure, there were any number of nay-sayers, but they were by and large excused as cranky malcontents. Bernard Levin of the *Times* was one, and *The Economist* was another.[11] One of the two Legislative Council members who did not endorse the agreement, John Swaine, argued that the British had lost Hong Kong years before the negotiations began. "[Britain] disabled itself a long time ago," he said, "when it closed the door to Hongkong . . . by a series of immigration and nationality acts which turned the Hongkong passport-holder into a second-class citizen. If you don't want them, how hard will you negotiate on their behalf?"[12] T. S. Lo, a long-time member of both the Executive and the Legislative Council, resigned in protest from both and promptly donated a large sum of money to help set up a non-profit organization for providing information on immigration possibilities for Hong Kong Chinese.

The Views of the People

Through it all, the views of the more than 5.5 million Chinese inhabitants of the colony remained largely obscured. Given Peking's undeniable claim to the New Territories, China's "right" to recover Hong Kong was not likely to be contested, and the Chinese inhabitants were relieved that some of the uncertainty had been removed. But most would doubtless have preferred to maintain the status quo, with all its faults and limitations.

Further masking any unease its people might have felt was their lack of familiarity with those mechanisms used in Western nations to exhibit popular feeling, such as demonstrations and petitions. Any voices raised in protest were therefore bound to be muffled. The ambivalence many felt was well expressed in a November 25 editorial in the Chinese-language paper *Ming Pao*:

> As a whole, it may be said that almost all the people in Hong Kong believe that Hong Kong is a part of China's territory, which explains why 80 per cent of the people interviewed believe that Hong Kong should be reverted to China in 1997. However, as most of the people have not been well impressed by the performance of the Chinese communists in the past, they tend to be sceptical about Hong Kong's status in the years to come. As to the agreement, a great majority of the people are very satisfied or quite satisfied with its contents. Yet there are still about half of the people interviewed, who are not reassured that the agreement will be faithfully implemented.[13]

In a cursory nod to Hong Kong public sentiment, an Assessment Office was set up to gather the people's views on the draft agreement. The office took out newspaper and television advertisements urging people to write to say whether they found the Joint Declaration acceptable—as a *package*. This was a critical point. The British had insisted that no alteration in the terms of the declaration was possible; it was strictly a take-it-or-leave-it deal. Naturally, this requirement immediately biased opinion in favor of the agreement, inasmuch as disagreement would leave the colony with no terms at all for 1997.

A number of respondents spoke of their disappointment. "It is difficult to foresee the future," wrote one man. "The draft agreement is a postdated cheque. The results can only be known when it is proved."[14] Another wrote:

> I belong to the middle income group who do not have the means to emigrate to other countries, and because I was born and educated in Hong Kong, I would wish to stay in Hong Kong. For the purpose of your statistics you can classify me as one of those who would accept the draft agreement, but I hope you will also take into account that I only accept it with much reluctance and with many reservations about the feasibility of its implementation. My heart is not truly at ease and I have no full confidence in our future. The whole thing has not been a very fair play to us because we have not had any say and there is no alternative other than not to have an agreement at all.[15]

Others were more critical, particularly on the sensitive issue of nationality. In Hong Kong, only a handful of inhabitants have full British passports, that is, passports that include the right of abode in the United Kingdom. Most residents have either British National (Overseas) passports or British Dependent Territories Citizens passports, neither of which includes the right of abode, or, for those immigrants from China who have not applied for British citizenship, simple Certificates of Identity. "With one stroke of the pen," complained one letter writer, "you have stripped us of our identity and slotted us into racial categories—an unforgivable act."[16]

Another contended that "Britain cannot simply rescind a historic and moral responsibility of looking after her subjects. These people are legally British and cannot be made stateless."[17] Especially bitter were those who had become naturalized as citizens and as such had sworn fidelity to the Crown. "I feel the oath of allegiance to the Queen to be very serious and am disillusioned by what the British government has done," said one.[18]

Perhaps a more reliable indicator of popular feeling than what was said by those who wrote to the Assessment Office is the number of people who didn't write. Of the 5.6 million people then living in Hong Kong, only about 2,500 sent in their opinions. The reason was not hard to discern. Many Hong Kongers, with their long experience with Chinese governments, worried about the confidentiality of their responses. At the outset the Assessment Office had maintained that all submissions had to include the writer's name and address to be considered. But this provoked a small furor, and the government then proposed sending all the collected responses to London for safekeeping for thirty years, after which time they might be made public. This announcement only inflamed anxiety, for Hong Kong people knew they would be living under Peking's rule when the submissions were finally made public. They wanted all the opinions destroyed after being processed.

For a short time it looked as though no one would write in. Then the government relented and agreed that all submissions would be burned once the Joint Declaration was ratified in 1985. Of course, a referendum would have been the easiest—and most accurate—way of ascertaining public opinion on the accord. But neither Britain nor China could risk that, for once the negotiations had reached the point where Britain surrendered sovereignty, securing the people's acceptance became more difficult.

In November 1984 the Assessment Office released its finding: "After the most careful analysis and consideration of all the information received, the office has concluded that most people of Hong Kong find the draft agreement acceptable."[19] However strained, this was exactly what Britain needed. The government had publicly stated some time before that it would not enter into any agreement with the Chinese that was not acceptable to the people of Hong Kong; it had to avoid at all costs the appearance of doing exactly what it did, which was to conclude an agreement over their heads and then force it down their throats.

The slide down the slippery slope had begun. Increasingly it seemed that the Joint Declaration was not intended to be honored as a treaty; it was, rather, a tactic to enable the British to retreat come 1997.

DIRECT ELECTIONS: YES OR NO?

Under the British system, the government puts forth a Green Paper to propose a certain policy, and public reaction is measured. Several months later it issues a White Paper, setting out and explaining the policy that has actually been adopted.

In July 1984, two months before the Joint Declaration was initialed, the government had issued a Green Paper entitled "The Future Development of Representative Government in Hong Kong." The Green Paper expressed the government's desire "to develop progressively a system of government the authority for which is firmly rooted in Hong Kong, which is able to represent authoritatively the views of the people of Hong Kong, and which is more directly accountable to the people of Hong Kong."[20] The Green Paper addressed the most controversial aspect of democracy, i.e., direct elections to the Legislative Council; here it noted that "suggestions have been made that direct elections to the Legislative Council based on a universal franchise should be introduced as soon as possible" and that "such arrangements are a standard feature of many democratic systems of government."[21] In short, the people of Hong Kong were led to believe that the Green Paper was mapping out the path to a directly elected legislature and that this was considered an important aspect of making the Joint Declaration work.

British officials had bolstered this impression with their own comments. On July 18, 1984, Sir Geoffrey had addressed the Commons. "Those proposals [of the Green Paper] are well designed to enhance the representative status of Hong Kong's Central Government institutions and to give the Hong Kong people a stronger voice in the administration of the territory in the years to come," he said. "The people of Hong Kong will now be putting forward their views, which will be taken into account in a subsequent White Paper."[22] He specifically spoke about elections to the Legislative Council in 1988 as well as 1991.

Two months later, after the ceremony in which the Joint Declaration was initialed, Sir Edward Youde, the governor of Hong Kong, flew back to the colony to preside over a special session of the Legislative Council. At this session, the governor said that the declaration had the endorsement of his Executive Council and of the Thatcher government in London. He again alluded not solely to the Joint Declaration itself—which promises a legislature "constituted by elections"—but to the direction mapped out in the Green Paper. The Joint Declaration, said Sir Edward, "will allow scope for the development of Hong Kong's governmental system as the years progress. As you know, our objective in the years *immediately ahead* is to use that process to root political power in the community where it belongs [emphasis added]."[23]

A few days later, on October 4, the governor returned to the Legislative Council. He acknowledged the interest in free elections elicited by the Green Paper, and the considerable support for "mov[ing] to direct elections by 1988."[24] The emphasis at the time, in Parliament and in the press, was that time was of the essence, that if Hong Kong were to adopt democracy successfully it was imperative to do so well before 1997 to give the colony time to develop its institutions and gain experience.

The November 1984 White Paper, "The Further Development of Representative Government in Hong Kong," though hailed as a step forward, was actually a slight retreat from the Green Paper issued earlier that year (which had been an important reason for the support given to the Joint Declaration, for it seemed to clarify some of the worrisome vagueness of the agreement). The White Paper ostensibly confirmed the need to institute democracy right away. But a note cited "considerable general public concern" that "too rapid progress toward direct elections could place the future stability and prosperity of Hong Kong in jeopardy."[25] The White Paper appeared on the eve of debate in Commons about the Joint Declaration, during which time Members underscored the need to move toward representative government with haste. George Robertson put his finger on the problem:

> The progress towards the more elected and representative government that is proposed in the White Paper is perhaps unduly cautious. The government of Hong Kong must be ready in the 1987 review to consider holding direct elections and having a greater proportion of directly elected legislators and extra members than they were willing to contemplate at the moment. The danger now is not of Chinese over-reaction to democratic reform but of insufficient time before 1997 in which to create a strong, viable, locally based system which will withstand the inevitable pressure and tremors as 1997 advances.[26]

Richard Luce, then minister of state with special responsibility for Hong Kong, was at pains to stress that the government and Parliament were in agreement on this critical issue:

The constitutional development of Hong Kong has caused great interest, and a large number of honorable members have expressed legitimate concerns. We all fully accept that we should build up a firmly based democratic administration in the years between now and 1997.[27]

Mr. Luce's opinion was reaffirmed by Baroness Young, speaking for the government in the Lords debate that followed less than a week later. "I fully accept the legitimate concerns which have been expressed that we should develop a solidly based democratic administration in Hong Kong in the period up to 1997."[28]

Taken as a whole, as they were meant to be taken, such comments led Parliament as well as the people of Hong Kong to believe that the guarantees of the Joint Declaration, within the context of the Green and the White Paper, would be put into place by a government in Hong Kong of the people, by the people, and for the people, long before the PRC resumed its claim of sovereignty. In short, China was to get Hong Kong but Hong Kong was to get democracy.

Britain Backs Down

The Achilles Heel in all this was twofold, a misunderstanding, first, of China, and second, of Communism. To ask for any agreement that continued the British presence was to ask for a formal sanction to which no Chinese leader, particularly no Chinese Communist leader, could ever assent. Hence the government's continuing defense, that it wangled the best agreement possible under the circumstances, even if true is beside the point. Even the relatively liberal Zhao Ziyang once remarked that if he had to choose between sovereignty and prosperity, he would choose sovereignty. Just as important, Communists approach treaties as merely tactical concessions, not strategic conclusions. For the 1984 accord to have had any chance of working required a firm commitment on the other side to hold Peking to the fine print.

British resolve survived less than a year. In November 1985 Michael Chugani reported in the *South China Morning Post* that China and Britain were at odds over interpretation of provisions of the Joint Declaration. Two days later, the director of the New China News Agency in Hong Kong, Xu Jiatun, gave a press conference in which he waved a copy of the Joint Declaration before reporters and intimated that someone was violating its terms by introducing change. (Mr. Xu was later to be blamed by Peking for the embarrassing demonstrations against the PRC in Hong Kong that included some of his own employees, and in 1990 he defected to the United States.) This was an attack on Britain's program to institute self-rule for the colony. Despite the Joint Declaration's unequivocal provision that Britain was to rule without interference from the mainland until 1997—ironically, the first official Communist acknowledgment of the legitimacy of any British rule in Hong Kong—Peking now insisted that political reforms be discussed at meetings of the Joint Liaison Group set up to handle implementation. It was a clear test of British will.

Instead of insisting on its right to govern Hong Kong for the next twelve years, Britain folded. A few weeks after Xu's press conference, Timothy Renton, minister of state with special responsibility for Hong Kong, was dispatched to the Chinese capital, where he introduced a new term that would come to haunt Hong Kong: "convergence." There was, Renton said, no moral commitment to introducing a Westminster system in Hong Kong. Hong Kong would best be served, the argument went, if its pre-1997 arrangement was close to its post-1997 one.

The consequence of this compliance was the establishment of a de facto China veto over Hong Kong's political development. No statements about this have ever been made public, but it is apparent from subsequent actions that Britain agreed to slow down plans for democratic reform. Since then Chinese demands on Britain have only escalated, and the governor, Sir

David Wilson, has been reduced to traveling hat in hand to Peking to seek the approval that was legally given him in the Joint Declaration.

The 1987 Green Paper

This capitulation was made manifest in 1987, the target date for a long-promised round of political reform. Again the government published a Green Paper. But unlike all previous Green Papers, this did not advocate any specific course of action. Rather, it presented Hong Kong people with a technical array of options. The government explained that it did not want to "lead public opinion." Hong Kong democrats thought otherwise. What London didn't want, they said, was to *find out* public opinion. The government, they charged, was deliberately aiming to confuse people.

In its Annual Report on Hong Kong to Parliament for 1985–86, the government had acknowledged that the issue attracting the "greatest attention" was "whether an element of direct elections should be introduced, and, in particular, whether they should be introduced in 1988."[29] But though it thereby conceded the importance of this issue, the government refused to hold a referendum on the question. In fact, it seemed to make every effort to obscure an up-or-down vote on the issue of direct elections by burying the matter under a mass of options and technical details.

Not once in the forty-two-page Green Paper was the question put squarely to the people: "Are you in favor of direct elections in 1988 or not?" On the contrary, people were asked to choose among a mind-boggling array of options. The description of the options, technical enough to confuse even an experienced U.S. citizen, was particularly ill suited to a public unfamiliar with the mechanics of democracy. Consider the options presented to Hong Kongers on just one point, the composition of their Legislative Council:

(i) to make no changes in the numbers and relative proportions of Official, Appointed, and Elected Members;

(ii) to conclude that direct elections to the Legislative Council are not desirable;

(iii) to conclude that, in principle, some element of direct elections is desirable, but that it should not be introduced in 1988;

(iv) if changes are desired in 1988, to choose one or more of the following options:

    (a) to increase slightly the number of Official Members;

    (b) to reduce the number of Appointed Members;

    (c) to increase the number of Members elected by the functional constituencies;

    (d) to increase the number of Members elected by the electoral college;

    (e) to introduce a directly elected element in addition to the existing systems of election, by means of either territory-wide or constituency-based elections;

    (f) to replace the system of indirect elections from the electoral college geographical constituencies by a system of direct elections.

This time the government established a Survey Office to gather views on the Green Paper, and that office hired the polling firm A.G.B. McNair H. K. to conduct two polls. In sharp contrast to the surveys conducted by other organizations in the colony, those prepared by A.G.B. McNair simply reproduced the tangled array of options and sub-options included in the Green Paper. Not surprisingly, the firm reported that only 12 to 15 per cent of the public favored direct elections in 1988.

This was not the full story. Given that at least ten surveys were carried out by other organizations during the same period of time, and that each of these found overwhelming support for the introduction of direct elections in 1988,

A.G.B. McNair's results take on a suspicious hue. In 1988 the *Far Eastern Economic Review* commissioned an independent appraisal of the government's surveys. Prepared by a former secretary general of Gallup International, Norman Webb, the study criticized the method and the questions. "It is readily apparent that they have either been obliged to, or voluntarily accepted, the task of conducting this combined survey operation within a strictly laid down format which did not as a result achieve its declared objective, that of finding out the wishes of the people of Hong Kong," it concluded.[30] Even the Survey Office's own findings revealed that between 40 and 43 per cent of those polled failed to understand the questions or said they had no opinion. Later, during the debate in Parliament, it was revealed that the managing director of A.G.B. McNair had confirmed that had he been given a free hand, the questions would have been worded differently. In short, the questions were deliberately rendered confusing to yield a sufficiently cloudy outcome that would justify the government's prior decision to defer direct elections until after 1988.

That was not the way the government put it, of course. When it issued the next White Paper in February 1988, the operative word was "stability." In Parliament Sir Geoffrey defended the postponement on the grounds that he had never specifically *promised* direct elections in 1988, in the manner of a divorce lawyer whose client suddenly decided he didn't want to give his wife the house after all. Nonetheless, the government announced that it had "decided to introduce a number of directly elected Members into the Legislative Council in 1991."[31] Ostensibly the decision was based on the findings of the Survey Office. But everyone knew that in this, as in so much else, one opinion loomed higher than all the 124,228 opinions the Survey Office had received. That opinion was Peking's.

To those unacquainted with Hong Kong, the difference between 1988 elections and 1991 elections might appear a technical point, a matter of pace rather than a choice between two very different outcomes. In reality, it was a litmus test of Britain's will to see the Joint Declaration through to the full in the time it had left to administer the colony. Peking opposed the introduction of direct elections in 1988 and pulled out all stops to defeat the measure, arguing through its institutions such as the Bank of China that elections were contrary to Hong Kong's interests. Putting off elections until 1991 would give the PRC time to finish and ratify the Basic Law, the mini-constitution that will set out the parameters of the possible in post-1997 political life. Thus the delay in introducing directly elected members to the Legislative Council until 1991 threatened the whole meaning of elections, depending on the substance of the Basic Law.

Today such fears have proved warranted. The Basic Law ratified by Peking in 1990 defines a legislature devoid of real power, making it largely irrelevant whether these members are ultimately to be elected by the Hong Kong people, appointed by Peking, or selected by lottery. And so, while the government had made a great deal of noise about democratic improvements and had taken pains to amass tens of thousands of opinions on the democratic preferences of the public, it then instituted them in such a way that they had no teeth, so as not to offend Peking.

Suggestions that only the Chinese version of the Basic Law will be legally binding further complicate the matter, especially in light of the peculiar ways in which Chinese authorities define such words such as "consult," "elections," and "voluntary." Had even *one* Legislative Council member been elected in 1988, he or she would have been in position to exert pressure to influence the Basic Law in a more democratic direction. That local member could have argued that he or she alone represented Hong Kong people in a way that appointed members—those from functional constituencies, foreign governors, Chinese bureaucrats, British civil servants, wealthy moguls, and the like—never could. Accordingly, elected council members were what China and Britain alike wanted least.

THE EXODUS

As usual the Hong Kong Chinese were the first to perceive the shift of power, long before the legions of foreign experts, international observers, and local apologists. One of the earliest signs of their new understanding of where the real power lay was that they stopped taking their grievances to the governor's residence. Traditionally, the Chinese people had gone to the top with their complaints. As they stopped going to Government House, they began to pay greater attention to the offices of the New China News Agency in Happy Valley—the de facto Chinese embassy in Hong Kong.

But the movement did not stop there. Increasingly the Hong Kong Chinese began to express their lack of confidence in the new arrangement the only way they knew how: with their feet. At first the outflow was little more than a trickle, and it was easily dismissed as the inevitable fall-off of old peasants who simply could not get it into their mulish heads that China had changed. It was hard to measure, too, inasmuch as the Hong Kong government did not keep figures on who left. The only way of estimating the outflow was through the number of Certificates of No Criminal Conviction issued by the Royal Hong Kong Police Force at a tiny, nondescript office on Shelter Street. These are relatively good figures, in that the certificates can be used only for immigration and are required by some forty-five countries to support immigrant visa applications. According to the Hong Kong government, the overwhelming majority of certificates were granted in support of applications for immigration to Canada, Australia, and the United States.

In the years up to and including 1985, the number of certificates issued hovered at about 20,000 a year. That figure soared to 35,600 in 1986, and to 52,000 in 1987. These certificates represent only adults and not minors, and only adults whose exit procedures are well under way; no one can ask for a certificate without a letter from the consulate of the country to which he or she has applied. Although the governor likes to say that outflows from Hong Kong are "normal," the dramatic increase each year suggests a panic just below the surface of this prosperous colony. Right or wrong, for better or worse, out of an accurate reading of the situation or blind fear, Hong Kong is in the midst of a massive flight of its most precious resource: its people.

So extensive has the exodus become that a whole new industry has been created around it. In typical entrepreneurial fashion, one man has launched a magazine called *The Emigrant*, printed in both Chinese and English and offering practical advice on immigration opportunities around the world. In every bookstall in the colony there is at least one shelf dedicated to such classics as *How to Get a Second Passport* and *The Immigration Code of the United States*. The personals section of the *Hongkong Standard* runs advertisements from Western men promising a passport in exchange for a pretty and passive bride. There is hardly a tea table in town that doesn't have someone talking either about his or her own plans to leave or about the newest loss of an acquaintance or relative or co-worker. Families have been split across continents—a sister to Sydney, a son to Vancouver, a father in Los Angeles—and there are sad tales of marriages breaking up, of handicapped children left behind, of children abandoning aged parents. The Western press refers to the Hong Kong exodus as the flight of the "yacht people," while locals refer to a man whose family has gone abroad as a *tai kong ren*, or astronaut, for all the time he spends in the air shuttling back and forth.

The Hong Kong government has only made matters worse, both by denying the exodus at first and by failing to address the reasons for it. As late as November 1987, two years after it had become obvious, Sir David Wilson was still saying there was no brain drain. "Are they all leaving and taking their money with them, as some of the international press have alleged?" the governor asked. "Hardly."[32] Subsequently he conceded that an outflow was indeed occurring but insinuated that this was nothing new, that Hong Kong has always had such a problem. This line of reasoning is easier to get away with abroad, where knowledge of Hong Kong remains scanty. (A controversial 1989 report on the brain drain by the U.S. consulate in Hong Kong appears as appendix A.)

The government has been reluctant to give an accurate accounting of how many people are leaving each year. At first authorities put the figures at 11,000 for 1985, 13,500 for 1986, and 27,000 for 1987.[33] But these figures are far below the numbers indicated by the Certificates of No Criminal Conviction (e.g., 52,000 in 1987). At least part of the explanation is that the government was measuring not actual emigration but net outflow. This is especially misleading in the case of Hong Kong now, inasmuch as most of those leaving are Hong Kong Chinese in search of another passport while those who take their places are by and large foreigners who are free to leave at any time.

Even conservative estimates show the government is fudging on the severity of the crisis. According to their own statistics, from January 1980 to June 1989—all *before* Tiananmen Square—the Royal Hong Kong Police issued 264,499 Certificates of No Criminal Conviction.[34] In other words, thousands more certificates have been issued than the government's immigration figures indicate.

These are by no means the only figures hinting at the disaster. The daily papers are filled with accounts of the flight of workers, often of experienced professionals. In the summer of 1989, for example, 120 engineers were lured away from Hong Kong Aircraft Engineering Company by Qantas Airways, to jobs that will give them the coveted Australian passports. ("If I offer them another HK$5,000 a month, does that substitute for passports?" asks Graham Howatt, Hong Kong Aircraft's managing director. "I think not.") Other governments actively assist those who decide to work for its nationals. "When we have people poached by, say, a French bank," says Citibank vice-president Frank Hawke, "you can bet that when this man goes to his new employer, sitting next to him will be an official from the French consulate."

Then there are the students. Between 1981 and 1987, the number those going abroad each year fluctuated between 10,000 and 13,000. In 1988 this figure rose to 15,026. As Paul Kwong argues in *The Other Hong Kong Report*, "although many [of these students] did return after a period of study, most did not."[35] Canada is the most popular destination for Hong Kong students, probably because of the relative ease of entry, and the number of student visas that country issues to Hong Kongers has been increasing dramatically. Also, many pregnant Hong Kong Chinese women are flying abroad to have their babies; a report in the *South China Morning Post* quotes one Canadian obstetrician as saying that passport babies account for three or four out of every ten births in his clinic.[36] The Hong Kong government itself has estimated that 435,664 people will leave the territory between 1989 and the end of 1997.

Most of the targeted countries have quickly recognized that Hong Kong's loss is their gain. Canada and Australia, to name two popular destinations, essentially offer passports for sale to Hong Kong Chinese investors. Not only has this given these host countries a growing source of new revenue; it also has meant an increased dynamism in their economies as they benefit from Hong Kong knowhow and experience. The United States, the most popular destination, has been slower to recognize these benefits, but the Immigration Act of 1990 (more will be said about this later) will help steer some Hong

Kong talent toward American shores. Even the Hungarian government has tried to woo the Hong Kong Chinese, offering citizenship in return for a $100,000 investment per head of household.[37]

All this is legal emigration. It does not even begin to get at the numbers of Hong Kong people leaving illegally. When U.S. forces invaded Panama in the spring of 1989, for example, they discovered a ring that helped provide Chinese people with phony U.S. passports; some Hong Kongers were found stranded in Panama after the invasion. Other rings were broken up in France and the Philippines. To this must be added the Hong Kong citizens who leave on tourist visas and don't return, either overstaying illegally or changing their visa status upon arrival in the host country.

These dismal trends are all confirmed by polling data showing that most people are at least thinking of getting out before the Communists get in. This was true well *before* Tiananmen Square. A January 1989 opinion poll conducted by Survey Research Hongkong showed that a third of Hong Kong's households had a member who either had a passport or was planning to get one. The figures were even worse for professionals, executives, and self-employed, reaching 46 per cent in that category.[38] A Federation of Hong Kong Industries Survey taken a short while afterward revealed that three out of four manufacturers are also planning to leave.[39]

The flight of capital is more difficult to track, but this movement of people does not occur in a financial vacuum. Economist George Hicks points out that even 100,000 people, taking with them an average of $500,000, would drain Hong Kong of about $50 billion—about the size of the colony's gross domestic product.

Because Hong Kong is so free and open, it has adapted to these changes and will adapt to future ones more readily than almost any other place on earth. But the effect is already being felt. The weekly flight out of more than 1,200 citizens, besides showing what Hong Kong Chinese really think of British and Chinese promises—a *South China Morning Post* cartoon lists the theme song of the colony as "Leaving on a Jet Plane"—has had a painful impact. Growth has slowed greatly, from 1987's 13.8 per cent and 1988's 7.4 per cent down to 2.5 per cent for 1989 and 2.4 per cent in 1990. Well before the tanks rolled into Tiananmen Square, the Hong Kong Chinese were packing their bags and pulling up roots, searching for that elusive peace and stability that Hong Kong, almost alone of Chinese societies, would still possess but for a fatal scratch of the pen on a turn-of-the-century treaty between two empires that no longer exist.

4

Tiananmen Square

FROM the first days of the colony, Hong Kong people have sustained an almost militant indifference to politics, content to cultivate the Confucian virtues, devote themselves to the advancement of their families, and leave the messy details of governing to the British. Not a small part of the reason most Chinese were in Hong Kong was to escape the political turmoil of the mainland, whether it was the dying Qing dynasty, the short-lived republic headed by Sun Yat-sen, the Japanese occupation, or the Communists. Their strange new overlords from the West were not hard to get along with. Unlike other forces that came to power in China—from Chiang Kai-shek to Mao Zedong—the British were fairly tolerant of traditional Chinese customs, the grosser practices such as foot-binding excepted, of course. And so, apart from periodic bursts of nationalism (which could be violent, as the Cultural Revolution showed), Hong Kong people kept their politics mostly to themselves. The British encouraged this attitude, for it made their rule in a tumultuous part of the world that much easier.

Local organizers were thus pleased when on December 4, 1988, some 5,000 or so people turned out at Victoria Park to participate in a march for democracy that would take them to the doorstep of the PRC's New China News Agency. The marchers on this slightly overcast day looked almost pathetically respectable: a few placards, row upon row of solid citizens, some mild sloganeering at the end. At the time it was the largest such demonstration for democracy the colony had ever seen. Although it did suggest there existed strong public sentiment on behalf of representative government, the Hong Kong government must have realized that it also showed how little the government had to fear from denying political reform.

When the Chinese year of the snake began two months later, in February 1989, Hong Kong's future seemed more or less fixed. The mainland Chinese were putting the finishing touches on the Basic Law, the mini-constitution that would govern the Special Administrative Region of Hong Kong once it was returned to Chinese rule in July 1997; the brain drain was proceeding apace; and optimists and pessimists continued to argue past each other. The pessimists believed that the decision to defer direct elections to after 1988 had doomed the colony, inasmuch as China would have already mapped out its plans for post-1997 Hong Kong without any pressure from true representatives of the Hong Kong people. The optimists, increasingly fewer outside the government payroll, merely repeated that the fears were unwarranted, arguing that whatever else the Chinese were they were practical people and therefore not about to kill the goose that lay the golden egg.

Among the more curious propositions put forth by this latter group was that the people's distrust of the PRC had to be discounted precisely *because* of their unhappy first-hand experience with the Communists. Sir Robert Adley, a conservative M.P. who has been one of the more vociferous friends of China, elevated his own judgment accordingly. "Maybe I am a dupe," he wrote in 1984, "but victims of unspeakable behavior cannot or will not believe that times have really changed. Of all things surely, Chinese are pragmatic: and pragmatism is an essential element in finding peaceful solutions to complex problems."[1] This same member would rise in Parliament a few years later to denounce those British subjects in Hong Kong who were seeking the equivalent of British rights for themselves; he described them as "trouble-makers" with "a vested interest in spreading unease."[2]

1989: A Short-Lived Spring

All these assumptions would be shattered in the course of a few short weeks in 1989 known as the Peking Spring. It was a period when new leaders unbeholden to either Britain or China struggled to articulate Hong Kong's own unique identity. Contrary to the official British line, the events of April–June 1989 did little to alter the facts surrounding Hong Kong's transition to Chinese rule. What they did was carve the issue in high relief and for the first time bring the associated problems home to the rest of the world.

Two forces were at work during the demonstrations at Tiananmen. One was Mikhail Gorbachev's trip to Peking, the first visit of a Soviet party leader to the Chinese capital. Up to then, established wisdom had had it that while the Chinese had done better by *perestroika*, the Soviets had pulled out ahead on *glasnost*. Gorbachev's visit thus was seized upon by demonstrators already out in the capital as a call for an opening on the political front. Some columnists even went so far as to compare George Bush unfavorably with his Soviet counterpart, inasmuch as the president's visit earlier that year had turned out to be something of a dud when Chinese officials prevented astrophysicist Fang Lizhi, China's leading dissident, from attending a dinner to which Bush had invited him.

The other, more important impetus for the Peking Spring was the death of Hu Yaobang, a party leader who had been purged after the 1986 student demonstrations were denounced as having been inspired by "bourgeois liberalism." Like Zhou Enlai, whose death in 1976 had spawned similar demonstrations on Tiananmen Square, Hu enjoyed a reputation as a reformer. His funeral provided an opportunity for mainlanders to take to the streets to air their gripes at the brake on liberalization announced earlier that spring at a party conference. "This is not just for Hu Yaobang," said Fang Lizhi. "This is a chance for students to let the government know they are unhappy with the present situation."[3]

Hu died on April 15. A small group of students then gathered on Tiananmen Square, boldly defying the government. They were ripe for protest. During the winter of 1986/87, their complaints about dormitory conditions, living standards, and the limited opportunities they would face after finishing their studies had set off the rebellion that ultimately led to Hu's ouster. These complaints had never been resolved, and the discontent had been fueled by a directive issued in March confirming that students would have to submit to having their jobs assigned to them after graduation.

These were decidedly self-centered concerns, and in an effort to give them a more idealistic gloss the students broadened their complaints to include calls for freedom of speech, freedom of the press, and an end to the official corruption that plagues this and all other Communist systems. On April 21, most Peking University students decided to boycott their classes, and the next day, the day of Hu's funeral, some 80,000 students massed on the square, petitioning the party leaders who were meeting inside the Great Hall of the People.

On April 24 Zhao Ziyang, the party's general secretary, considered sympathetic to the students, left China for a visit to North Korea. With him out of the way Deng Xiaoping convened a meeting of the Politburo's Central Committee. There he called for a forceful editorial that would brand the protestors as anti-socialist elements who had been influenced by events in Eastern Europe; this would be followed by a crackdown. The next issue of the *People's Daily* accordingly featured an article with Deng's imprimatur, blaming Fang and the other dissidents for provoking the demonstrations. The editorial was read aloud over television news broadcasts, and many Chinese noted that it employed the same language used in 1986/87 when Hu was ousted.

This time it backfired. Far from frightening the students, the editorial only inflamed the opposition. Intellectuals and workers began to line up behind the protesting students. The mood was electric. To a people very conscious of history, the closeness to the seventieth anniversary of the May 4th Movement—when the Chinese rose up against foreign domination by Japan and warlord rule, a date akin to the Fourth of July for Americans — further excited expectations. Zhao, now back from North Korea, delivered a conciliatory speech to the students, urging restraint.

On May 15, with the students still occupying the square and public feeling against Deng running high, Gorbachev arrived in Peking. Two days earlier the students had begun a hunger strike, which lifted morale and brought the citizens of Peking out in solidarity. For the first time, students and workers were publicly united in their criticism of the government. Party leaders took it as an ominous sign: with the ouster of Communist strongmen from all over Eastern Europe fresh in their minds, they were determined to avoid the same fate. When the protestors defied orders to clear the square for Gorbachev's visit, the arrival ceremony was switched to the airport, and the Soviet leader's visits to the Monument to the Martyrs of the Revolution (on the square) and the Forbidden City (at the top of the square) were canceled. It was a monumental loss of face.

On May 18, sensing the danger, the government agreed to meet with the students. Before television cameras a pajama-clad student leader from Peking's Teachers' University gave Premier Li Peng a dressing down. The next day Zhao came to the square to meet with the students in tears. "I came too late, too late," he said. It would be his last public appearance. At midnight the next day, Premier Li addressed cadres from the

Party, the government, and the army, denouncing the "turmoil" in the capital and calling for harsh measures to restore order. Martial law was imposed, and the students were ordered to vacate the square by 5 A.M. May 22.

Again the government's move only emboldened the protestors, particularly since the troops sent in to clear the square were unarmed and clearly reluctant to use force. They were overwhelmed by the people, who threw up roadblocks and swarmed around convoys. On May 30, a Goddess of Democracy, cast in the image of America's Statue of Liberty, arose as a counter to Mao's portrait. The protestors had the square, though they weren't sure quite what to do with it.

Hong Kong Shows Solidarity

Their cousins in Hong Kong watched with keen interest. The Peking Spring meant almost as much to them as it did to those on the mainland, for people had begun to realize that how Hong Kong would look come 1997 depended on what kind of China there was in 1997. Acutely conscious that they lacked the same democratic guarantees absent on the Communist mainland, and that they were not going to get them under the current British government, the people of Hong Kong decided to raise their own Goddess of Democracy.

The consequences were spectacular. In a colony not given to public demonstrations, more than a million people turned out twice in one month to express solidarity with their compatriots in Tiananmen Square. The series of demonstrations began with some smaller rallies, such as one on May 20 in which 40,000 people braved Typhoon Brenda to show their support for the demonstrators in Peking. The next day almost a million people marched on the New China News Agency offices. A sign was raised saying "Today's China Is Tomorrow's Hong Kong." The following two Sundays witnessed similar rallies, culminating in a twelve-hour fund-raising pop concert.

In scope, in size, in fervor, these demonstrations were unprecedented. They transformed Hong Kong. Long known as one of the rudest places in the world, Hong Kong in protest showed a courteous face. There was almost no shoving or pushing. People waited for others to get off buses and trains before boarding. As the Hong Kong government's yearbook conceded, although the volume of people in the streets was "unprecedented" and caused monumental inconvenience to the public at large, the protests "did not significantly affect public order."

At a marathon concert at a racecourse, collections raised more than $1.5 million for those camping out in Tiananmen Square. Twenty-four-year-old Frances Heung spoke for many in the colony: "I am a Chinese British subject with a British passport, but what does that mean? Nothing. I cannot leave Hong Kong. The people in Tiananmen Square are my brothers and sisters. They have the same blood as I do. I am Chinese."[4] Even when passions were running highest in the weeks to follow, after the tanks rolled into Tiananmen, Hong Kongers maintained their dignity and poise. The Peking Spring had forced them into a cold re-examination of their own identity and future.

The Tiananmen Crackdown

The weeks of occupation of Tiananmen lulled people into a false sense of invincibility. Although students openly talked about martyrdom ("Only when the square is washed in our blood will people of the whole country wake up,"[5] said student leader Chai Ling in her last, taped speech), they nonetheless were taken by surprise when the guns were finally turned on them. On the day on which the crackdown would later occur, the front page of Hong Kong's leading newspaper reported only a "scuffle" with troops and said the crowd was yelling "the People's Liberation Army loves the people." Party leaders seemed impotent to enforce their will.[6]

No one was more surprised by the crackdown than Hong Kong. When the people awoke on June 4 to headlines of "Beijing Bloodshed" and photos of the grisly turmoil, hundreds of thousands again rushed to the streets to show their anger and dismay. The two main leaders of the pro-democracy movement in Hong Kong, Szeto Wah and Martin Lee, announced they were suspending their work on the Basic Law Drafting Committee. (Later, Communist authorities booted them off the committee for good.) The march that day was sponsored by the Hongkong Alliance in Support of the Patriotic Democratic Movement in China. Throughout the two-and-a-half-hour assembly, the participants chanted "Down with Li Peng," calling him "butcher," "fascist," and "Adolf Hitler." Citizens queued up outside the Red Cross office to donate blood for the injured in Peking. The *South China Morning Post* editorialized that Peking's "ten years of winning confidence through its 'open door' policies and economic reform have been wasted in one night of slaughter."[7] Across the front of the I. M. Pei–designed Bank of China—Asia's tallest building, built as a symbol of the mainland's confidence in Hong Kong's post-1997 future—protestors draped a banner with a grim message: "Blood Must Be Paid with Blood."

The reaction of London and Peking, the two powers determining Hong Kong's future, was instructive. Peking's first priority, of course, was restoring the government's authority in China. But before long party leaders turned some of their attention to the soon-to-be-acquired territory, noting as they did how deeply the demands for greater freedoms voiced at Tiananmen Square resonated throughout Hong Kong. It had not escaped their notice that the demonstrations in Hong Kong had included employees from Communist-run organizations, from the Bank of China to the Hong Kong Federation of Trade Unions and the New China News Agency itself. Hong Kong's newspapers, almost all of which (even the normally pro-China ones such as *Wen Wei Po*) had sided with the protestors, were denounced by name in the official Chinese media. In his report to the National People's Congress on the government's crackdown, the mayor of Peking, Chen Xitong, pointed to the detailed news coverage from Hong Kong as evidence that the students were "in collusion with foreign forces" to force China "to give up the socialist road."[8]

The prospect of ruling a people accustomed to freedom frightened PRC officials, and the notion that Hong Kong was "polluting" China with its market ways became a frequent mainland theme over the next few months. On July 11, 1989, the Party's new general secretary, Jiang Zemin, told leading members of the Basic Law Drafting Committee and the Basic Law Consultative Committee that "we practice our socialism and you may practice your capitalism. 'The well water should not interfere with the river water.' "[9] In the wake of Tiananmen, former president Ronald Reagan had told a crowd at Oxford, "You can't massacre an idea," and Chinese party leaders feared he was right. Time and again the Communist authorities made it clear they would not permit Hong Kong to become a "revolutionary base" for activities against the motherland.

Outright intimidation soon followed. Although they were not mentioned by name, Szeto Wah and Martin Lee, the two main pro-democracy leaders in Hong Kong, found themselves branded subversives in the official *People's Daily*. Their coalition, the Alliance in Support of the Patriotic Democratic Movement in China, likewise was condemned, and a delegate of that alliance, Lee Cheuk-yan, was arrested in Peking (he was later released). That Hong Kong people turned to Britain for succor—Baroness Lydia Dunn asked for full British nationality for the 3.25 million British passport-holders in the colony, saying they were loyal subjects of the Crown—further enraged Peking.

The most forthright action orchestrated from Peking came within the considerable mainland apparatus functioning in the colony. Li Zi-song, the publisher of the Hong Kong–based Chinese Communist paper *Wen Wei Po*, was sacked. Not a party member himself, Li had nonetheless been a faithful fellow traveler for more than four decades, until the day *Wen Wei Po* expressed sympathy for the students on Tiananmen and derided the Peking regime as "fascist." The move confirmed what had long been suspected about these organizations with ties to the mainland: that control ultimately rested with Peking and not the nominal managers. A *People's Daily* editorial minced no words: "We shall not allow people to use Hong Kong for subverting the central people's government. Not engaging in activities to overthrow [the Chinese government] is a precondition for allowing [Hong Kong] to retain its capitalist system."[10]

Britain's Intensified Obligation

The obvious willingness of party chieftains to shoot down their own unarmed citizens suggested to an apprehensive Hong Kong that these same Chinese leaders would not be overly concerned about the fine points of the Joint Declaration. As the passions over June 4 subsided, Hong Kong people, knowing they soon would be living under Peking's rule, therefore became increasingly unwilling to engage in potentially suicidal confrontations. Given the predicament, the onus fell on the British government of Hong Kong to make the case for them. If Hong Kong was to survive the raising of the red flag, its institutions needed to be shored up to withstand the buffeting they would inevitably receive. Alone among the key players in the colony's future, Britain held the power to make things better.

Initial signs were encouraging. Alas, the mood didn't last. China's actions signaled Hong Kong that the situation was serious; Britain's feeble response told them it was also hopeless. Had Mrs. Thatcher and Sir David seemed inclined to side with their own people over Peking during the four years since the signing of the Joint Declaration, things might have been different. As it was, British post-Tiananmen assurances were convincing mainly to foreigners who didn't have to worry much about 1997 or those who had not been in the colony for years. They did little to reassure Hong Kong Chinese.

The British government in its annual report for 1989 could not even bring itself to attribute blame for the massacre; the chronology refers only to "the tragic events in Beijing." Indeed, the government's failure to report honestly the developments in the territory moved some Hong Kongers to put out an alternative yearbook for 1990, *The Other Hong Kong Report*, edited by T. L. Tsim and published by the Chinese University Press. The essays in this book give a far more accurate and far less sanguine picture than that offered by the official report. In Washington, Britain's ambassador, Sir Antony Acland, stated one week before the bloodshed that China "knows the importance of maintaining confidence,"[11] this at a time when Peking's leaders had already imposed martial law. On May 23 Hong Kong's secretary for economic services, Anson Chan, told a group of U.S. businessmen in Washington that jitters over 1997 were "blown out of proportion."[12]

Britain's actions *during* the massacre are no more defensible. Hong Kongers in Peking at the time (carrying British passports) reported that they were denied the protection of the British embassy. At a press conference in Washington a few weeks later, Yau Suk-yi disclosed that a group of Hong Kong Chinese in Peking had called the British embassy there after the killings. There were about forty of them, including a dozen or so reporters, and they considered themselves in grave danger, all the more so because they were not readily identifiable as foreigners. They faxed the embassy a list of names and their Hong Kong I.D. numbers. The British embassy called back a few hours later, telling them to get a taxi to the airport and a ticket back to Hong Kong. The Hong Kongers said that this would be impossible and that it was dangerous to stay in the hotel; they asked for transportation to the embassy. Embassy officials said there were no cars and no drivers. The Hong Kongers offered to walk. They were told there were no facilities to receive them. Jo-Jo Tam, a Hong Kong teacher, went to the embassy, got no assistance, and then went to the U.S. embassy, where she was helped.

In Hong Kong, the governor avoided any hint of criticism. "It is a time for sad and sober reflection," he said.[13] Mrs. Thatcher was similarly non-committal. "Britain will continue to stand by its commitment to a secure future for Hong Kong," she said. "And we are confident the Chinese government will continue to abide by their obligations under the 1984 agreement."[14]

For Hong Kong people the litmus test of Britain's "commitment" to them was simple: full passports. But Sir Geoffrey Howe, then foreign secretary, quickly dismissed this idea. In Commons on June 6, while blood was still fresh on Tiananmen Square, he made Britain's position clear:

> We share the desire of the House to do everything we can to enhance the security of the people of Hong Kong. On that basis, the Government are looking urgently and sympathetically at the scope for flexibility. But the House will appreciate the reason *why we could not easily contemplate a massive new immigration commitment which could more than double the ethnic minority population of the United Kingdom* [emphasis added].[15]

It was a revealing statement. (The full text is printed as appendix B.) The foreign secretary objected to the potential immigration not on the basis of sheer numbers but on the basis of race: Hong Kongers might double the minority population of the United Kingdom.

When Sir Geoffrey journeyed to Hong Kong a month later to attempt to boost sagging confidence, he was roundly jeered, unprecedented behavior by Hong Kong Chinese toward visiting British dignitaries. "You have no stauncher friend than Britain," he tried to tell them, but the chant of "Howe Go Home" showed they were not buying. One protestor's sign summed up the feeling of many: "The issue is right or wrong, not white or Wong."[16]

The Kowtow Continues

Other incidents continued the long kowtow that Britain had begun in 1985. In an October 1989 letter to the Chinese authorities, the political advisor of the Hong Kong government assured mainland leaders that Her Majesty's government was well aware of what was and was not to be tolerated in Hong Kong:

> The Hong Kong Government has no intention of allowing Hong Kong to be used as a base for subversive activities against the People's Republic of China. NCNA [New China News Agency] will have noticed the arrest of members of the April 5th Action Group outside their National Day reception. They will also have noted that . . . the Hong Kong Government has recently rejected a proposal for a permanent site for a replica statue of Democracy. No group in Hong Kong has more tolerance than the law allows. The Hong Kong Government will continue to have a prudent regard for the special circumstances of Hong Kong and the interests and concerns of the Chinese government.[17]

Two months later, the Television and Entertainment Licensing Authority chopped some sixteen minutes from a film called *Mainland China 1989*. The deleted section featured interviews with Chinese student leaders Wang Dan and Wuerkaixi and dissidents Fang Lizhi and Li Shuxian. The Licensing Authority invoked the Film Censorship Ordinance, arguing that the deleted segment was likely "to seriously damage good relations with other territories." It was not the first such occurrence;

two years earlier, Frank Ching had exposed in the *Asian Wall Street Journal* the Hong Kong government's long-time practice of censoring films that China might have found offensive. In July 1991 the Hong Kong government again did Peking's dirty work when it detained at Kai Tek airport eight overseas Chinese students who had valid visas. They were held upon arrival to prevent them from participating in a pro-democracy conference. A New China News Agency official said Hong Kong's decision was based on "promises" Britain had made to China.

In pre-Tiananmen Hong Kong, this might have been defensible as diplomatic *realpolitik*. In the post-Tiananmen context, the British reaction took on a more sinister hue. The intent seemed no longer to be to avoid gratuitous offense of Hong Kong's neighbor but to stifle potential dissent. The censorship of films sent a chilling message to the Hong Kong community: censor yourself before it comes to this.

Those to whom the message was directed were not slow to take the hint. In June, Hong Kong's two television stations decided not to broadcast a U.S.-produced video that supported the pro-democracy movement on the mainland. Tina Liu, a popular Hong Kong singer who helped produce the video, said she was told that the lyrics and shots were "not suitable." Later the government banned the screening of a Canadian film about a Chinese emperor who suppressed intellectuals to maintain his grip on power many dynasties ago; although it had nothing to do with Tiananmen Square, the British apparently wanted to spare Deng Xiaoping any potential embarrassment.

The hope was that a moderate tone would reassure a jittery mainland. In fact, the result of Britain's continued acquiescence was a widening spiral of incidents in which the Chinese continually raised the stakes. The most aggressive action came in May 1990, when Chinese military forces violated Hong Kong's waters and kidnapped at gunpoint five Hong Kong seamen and two policemen. The men had been out in a sting operation to crack a smuggling ring that was stealing cars in Hong Kong and sneaking them across the border; to their surprise, the smugglers turned out to be uniformed Chinese security officials, who abducted them. The two policemen were released within sixteen hours, but the five men working on the Hong Kong tug were held in a Shekou jail for twenty-seven days. Although the British had photographs indisputably showing the Chinese military officers acting in Hong Kong waters, they refused to make them public. According to an account in the *Far Eastern Economic Review*, this was by no means the only such confrontation: a government source said there had been at least twenty such incursions into Hong Kong waters, with the Chinese displaying "increasing belligerence."[18]

In what was clearly another attempt to satisfy Peking, the government prosecuted five pro-democracy advocates for using bullhorns in public. The five, all members of the United Democrats of Hong Kong, had been leading a rally at the Star Ferry around the time the final draft of the Basic Law was about to be released. They were on charged under a 1933 law designed to curtail unnecessary noise, but the real motive obviously was to convince China that Britain was looking out for its interests. In the end the men were convicted on two counts each (using the bullhorns without a permit and collecting funds without a permit) and fined HK$75 (about $10) on each count.

But the trial quickly became a cause célèbre and something of an embarrassment, particularly when the men said they would rather go to jail than pay the fine. A potentially explosive climax was avoided when someone—it is not known who—paid the fines for the convicted democrats (in Hong Kong, a person's fines can be paid by someone else). Significantly, the law was not enforced again during the trial, when demonstrators supporting the five men deliberately used bullhorns outside. And the five ultimately had their earlier convictions reversed on appeal. But the signal had been sent.

A Bill of Rights

All this has been accompanied by a massive cave-in on the political front. Until Tiananmen Square, it was relatively easy for the British to cut deals and let the promises laid out in the Joint Declaration and the associated Green and White papers slide. But once the tanks had done their job it became almost impossible for the Hong Kong government to argue that Hong Kong's best bet was to trust Deng Xiaoping (though, ironically, it has since returned to that line).

In the immediate aftermath, Sir Geoffrey promised that the government would accelerate the process of democratization and enact a bill of rights. This latter was intended as a means of firming up the protections Hong Kongers have become accustomed to—a crucial point, inasmuch as those freedoms are not guaranteed by law. The British further promised to reconsider the nationality question, on a limited scale. This kind of talk led even critics of the government to believe that Tiananmen Square might finally have spurred the British to take a more resolute stance toward China.

Such hopes soon proved illusory. True, the British did propose that People's Liberation Army troops not be stationed in post-1997 Hong Kong, that the power to declare a state emergency be vested in the post-1997 chief executive of Hong Kong (and not Peking)—a critical provision, in light of Tiananmen—and that the Chinese reconsider their opposition to a democratized Hong Kong. The governor himself traveled to the mainland to press for these provisions. But he did not *fight* for them, and again China prevailed through sheer force of will.

To its credit, the government did adopt a Bill of Rights, which was supposed to enshrine the key provisions of the

International Covenant on Civil and Political Rights. Despite complaints from across the border and hints that it might be repealed in 1997, the Legislative Council gave its blessing to a draft version, two years after the massacre. But this Bill of Rights excludes two of the main provisions of the International Covenant: the right to self-determination and the right to elect political representatives. The local Bar Association called it "limping and castrated."[19]

Even this watered-down version will be next to impossible to enforce. To begin with, China is not a party to the International Covenant. It has neither to comply with its provisions nor to submit periodic reports to the U.N.'s Human Rights Committee, the body charged with monitoring implementation. There was also the question whether the Bill of Rights would have supremacy over other laws in Hong Kong (as it does in, say, the United States), and whether it would be entrenched within Hong Kong's legal system, as Attorney General Jeremy Matthews promised in October 1989. Again the government came in at less than its word. Given that the Bill of Rights will expire with the rest of Britain's legislation, and inasmuch as final interpretation of the Basic Law rests in Peking and not Hong Kong, protections offered by the Bill of Rights are not likely to win out in any serious clash. For most Hong Kong people, the Bill of Rights is just another legalism. If China is not honoring the Joint Declaration today, what possible reason is there to believe it will honor the Bill of Rights when it assumes full control in 1997?

The one area in which Britain did move in the right direction was passports, though again it has been a matter of too little too late. It had long been my contention that full passports for *all* Hong Kongers ought to have been the cornerstone of British policy from the outset, even before the Joint Declaration, inasmuch as this was the only action that would have given Hong Kong people some leverage over their future overlords. This position has been steadfastly propounded by the *Asian Wall Street Journal* since 1984. In Britain it may be looked at as an invitation to immigration, but Hong Kongers see it as the opposite: an insurance policy that gives people a reason to *stay*. The overwhelming majority of Hong Kong people like their lives in Hong Kong and would prefer to remain where they are. All they are asking for is some security for themselves and their families against the worst. The refusal to grant this insurance policy casts doubt on the British government's credibility: if the future of Hong Kong is as bright as Whitehall says it is, Britain need not worry about any massive influx of Hong Kongers. In the wake of Tiananmen Square, advertisements making just this point began cropping up in the local press (see appendix C).

In legal terms, London's obligation here does not extend to all the 5.8 million residents of Hong Kong but only to the 3.25 million who are British citizens. Although these people have British passports, they do not have the right to live in Britain, which makes Britain the only country in the world to issue passports that do not give bearers the right of abode in the issuing nation. This situation makes Hong Kong passport-holders literally second-class citizens. It is difficult not to suspect race as a motivating factor, particularly since the British passports issued to the white subjects of Gibraltar and the Falklands (not to mention a million or so white South Africans) do include the right of abode in Britain.

Hong Kong's anomaly is all the more embarrassing when compared to nearby Macau, the Portuguese colony that reverts to Chinese rule in 1999. There Lisbon issued full passports to all its 100,000 holders. The British defend themselves by pointing out the difference in volume between recognizing 100,000 and 3,000,000 passports. But the practice still makes Britain unique within the European Community. France, for example, granted full citizenship to some 350,000 residents of its Pacific territories. And because Portugal is now a member of the European Community, residents of Macau with

Portuguese passports will be able to live in Britain while residents of Hong Kong with British passports cannot. For all these reasons, Martin Lee, chairman of the United Democrats, refers to the British Nationality Acts as the "Hong Kong Exclusion Acts" because this colony is the only one left out.

Whatever the reason, it cannot be economic. Hong Kong possesses a young, talented, entrepreneurial population who would prove a boon to any country they entered. In July 1989 the *South China Morning Post* published a study produced by the Hong Kong/U.K. Economy Research Group that took the worst-case scenario: all 3.2 million people leaving Hong Kong for Britain. The study, nicknamed "The Corry Report" (after Bernard Corry, a professor of economics at the University of London), concluded that on the whole the influx would benefit Britain, improving its balance of payments, boosting growth, reviving inner cities, and generally relieving the stress on social spending with an increase in the base working population. The results were all the more telling in that the researchers had begun with the opposite assumptions. "Our calculations came as a surprise to most of the members of the team writing this report," states the introduction. "Typically they had expected the outcome to be far more costly than these figures show."

However much Britain's continued exclusion of its Hong Kong Chinese citizens may be argued in terms of numbers, its fundamental mean-spiritedness comes through in the treatment of those who have sacrificed much for the Crown, such as the seventeen widows of men who died for the British Empire fighting the Japanese in World War II. The widows' case has been argued for years by British veteran Jack Edwards. Among the seventeen is Doris Kotwall, whose husband Jimmy was beheaded by the Japanese occupation forces in August 1944 for his work in the underground British Army Aid Group; he is buried near his brother—executed a year earlier for the same reason—in Stanley Military Cemetery. In his last letter from prison, written just before he was led to his execution, the banker-turned-resistance-leader urged his twenty-four-year-old wife to take heart. "Do not feel sorry for my death," he wrote. "I die with love in my heart for my family, my country, and relatives and friends."

Most of these women are in their seventies or eighties today. They would be unlikely to go to Britain even if they were granted citizenship. They want it only as reassurance and a sign of respect for their husbands. Even more than the government's political decisions about democracy, petty actions such as this have convinced Hong Kongers they are on their own.

Indeed, the only issue Hong Kongers now really care about is restoration of their rights as British citizens. While working at the *Asian Wall Street Journal* in the mid-1980s, I found that virtually every letter to the editor that came across my desk focused on the hated second-class passports, and in the immediate aftermath of Tiananmen Square there was a renewed effort for justice on this score. Almost all pro–Hong Kong groups joined the lobbying effort for passports.

There were signs that London was considering action on the passport issue—but never on the scale of granting the right of abode in Britain to all 3.25 million passport-holders. Instead, then foreign secretary John Major announced to the United Nations in September 1989 that the government had decided on "a package to encourage people essential to Hong Kong's future stability and prosperity to stay there, by giving them guarantees of resettlement in England if they wish. That package will be designed not to strip Hong Kong of its people, but to give them hope and confidence to remain."

Three months later Mrs. Thatcher released her plan: full passports to no more than 50,000 families, which under the standard immigration assumption would mean about 150,000 people. Most of the new passports will be granted to businessmen, managers, and top-ranked entrepreneurs, with the rest going to other professionals: doctors, accountants, nurses, teachers, lawyers, and people in sensitive jobs "serving Hong-kong or United Kingdom interests."

In the end, only 65,674 people turned in applications for the 50,000 slots, though the government had printed a million application forms. The reasons for the shortfall were varied. Complexity was a big one: the BN(HK)1 form was thirty-two pages long; the Guidance Notes ran to another eight pages; the General Guide was twenty-eight pages; and on top of this were reference manuals, some running into the hundreds of pages, dealing with more specific instructions still. No doubt distrust and preference also played a part. Anyone who could get through all these pages probably qualified for emigration to Canada, Australia, or the United States—without having to put his or her name on a British list that might some day find its way to China. Finally, the tiny number of passports offered sent its own message. "The British offer of 50,000 passports to keep key people in place here never even came close," said Paul Kwong, a demographer at the Chinese University in Hong Kong. "It was always too small for its stated goals."[20] In addition, those who did apply were told they would learn whether they had a passport in two years—an odd time period if the intention really was to shore up confidence now. Hong Kong democrats suggest the reason for the delay is that authorities hope applicants will have been accepted somewhere else in the meantime.

The Basic Law

At the same time that Britain was pushing this very limited insurance policy through its own Parliament, it was backtracking on the political reassurances given in the days following the June 4 bloodshed in China. In January 1990, the Basic Law Drafting Committee (minus Messrs. Lee and Szeto, who had been expelled by China in November 1989 for their pro-democracy advocacy) put forth the final draft of the mini-

constitution that will govern the post-1997 Special Administrative Region of Hong Kong. The Basic Law turned out to
be as bad as everyone had expected, and the British only made
it worse. By delaying Hong Kong's Bill of Rights until *after*
the Chinese had finalized the Basic Law, the British effectively
allowed the same men who had spilt blood on Tiananmen
Square to decide the degree of freedom that is to survive the
transfer of sovereignty in 1997.

The English-language version of the Basic Law has 160
articles, three annexes, and an appendix covering virtually
every aspect of Hong Kong life in a booklet sixty-nine pages
long. Like most constitutions, the Basic Law is an impressive
compendium of rights to be enjoyed by the affected persons,
the residents of Hong Kong. Like the 1984 Joint Declaration,
moreover, it includes reassuring general principles, e.g., that
"the socialist system and policies shall not be practised" in
Hong Kong, that Hong Kong will be allowed "a high degree
of autonomy," and that "the laws previously in force in Hong
Kong, that is, the common law, rules of equity, ordinances,
subordinate legislation and customary law shall be maintained." So much for the good. The problem is that the
political structure responsible for guaranteeing these freedoms
makes them highly unlikely.

The real meaning of the Basic Law was immediately apparent. When the mainland delegation brushed aside Hong Kong
concerns in its final draft of the Basic Law in January 1990—
before Britain published its promised Bill of Rights—it was a
signal that in the run-up to 1997 Britain would have nominal
authority but real power would lie with China. The February
1, 1990, cover of the *Far Eastern Economic Review* captured
this nicely with a drawing of the governor, the British foreign
secretary, and Mrs. Thatcher carrying white flags. The illustra-
tion was based on the historic photograph of the British
surrender of Singapore to the Japanese in 1942. In this case
the Basic Law constituted the new terms of surrender. "Gen-

eral Yamashita was amazed at the ease with which he acquired Singapore," said the magazine. "Li Peng may feel the same."[21]

In justifying their acquiescence, the British hearkened back to "convergence," the 1985 term that had gradually supplanted any plans for enforcing the terms and spirit of the Joint Declaration. The idea was that pre-1997 Hong Kong should converge as closely as possible with post-1997 Hong Kong. On paper it seems reasonable, but in reality it has had disastrous consequences for Hong Kong. "Convergence" theory means that, rather than pressing Peking to make the Basic Law converge with the Joint Declaration, Britain gave China veto power over political developments in the colony up to the transfer. This itself is a blatant violation of the Joint Declaration's provision that Britain was to continue to administer Hong Kong without interference in the years between the signing of the 1984 accord and 1997.

The British have tried to put the best face on this by pointing to China's "concessions." Upon closer examination, however, these concessions amount to little more than a promise to be more subtle in the future about their violations of the Joint Declaration. In that 1984 document, China had agreed to accept a legislature "constituted by elections"; whereas in the Basic Law it conceded to allowing a third of the legislature to be democratically elected by 1997. Not until the year 2003 will half the legislature be democratically elected, and there is no guarantee that the process will ever be extended to cover a majority of seats. Given the way the PRC has stacked the political deck, such an extension would be highly unlikely; if it did somehow take place, it would almost certainly occur under conditions that would make the elections irrelevant (e.g., if the power in Hong Kong is all retained by the chief executive acting in concert with the Standing Committee of the National People's Congress in Peking). Think of it this way: can anyone imagine offering Russians or East Europeans *half* a legislature in ten years and hailing that as representative government?

The other mainland "concession" was to limit the split-voting scheme to private members' bills. In plain language this means that legislators who have not been popularly elected can block the wishes of those who have been so elected. Naturally the reverse is not so. The net effect is to limit the powers of the democratically elected legislators (those who would presumably reflect the wishes of the Hong Kong people) while vesting more power in those not elected. Coming as it does on top of an arrangement already biased in favor of a strong chief executive, it further strengthens the mainland's hand in the colony's post-1997 affairs and relegates the Joint Declaration's promises of "a high degree of autonomy" to the historical dustbin.

The Airport Flap

In the end, the formal abandonment of the terms of the 1984 Joint Declaration came over a most unlikely issue: an airport. More precisely, this was the ambitious $16.3 billion Port and Airport Development Strategy announced in October 1989, which was intended to restore the confidence sapped by Tiananmen Square and give the governor something positive to talk about in his travels abroad. Alas, China started sniping at the project almost from the start, putting the Hong Kong government in a bind: if it went ahead with the project, it would risk bad relations with Peking; if it gave in, this would further erode confidence (especially investor confidence) in Britain's ability to govern.

Ostensibly the sticking point was the price tag. Experts agreed that Hong Kong's Kai Tek Airport will reach peak capacity by 1994 at the latest, and China never contested the need for a new airport. Dating from 1925, Kai Tek was bombed by the Japanese the same day as Pearl Harbor, rebuilt during the Occupation, bombed again by the Allies, and rebuilt again by the British. A landing at Kai Tek gives a good taste of the colony's cramped conditions: the plane swoops so low over neighboring housing estates that a passenger feels he could gather up the laundry drying on poles protruding from the windows. In a year the Kai Tek's single runway services almost 20 million passengers, and there is simply no room to expand.

The Chinese objected to the cost. They saw in the airport project yet another attempt by foreign imperialists to drain Chinese resources (Hong Kong's reserves are officially secret but have been estimated at $9.4 billion) before they leave, in this case by awarding fat contracts to British and American construction firms. The Chinese argument is that they do not want to find themselves stuck with a huge tab for these projects after Britain is gone.

Whatever the true concern, China quickly transformed the airport into a test of political control. For twenty months Peking emphasized that it alone could speak for the people of Hong Kong and that it consequently demanded (in defiance of the Joint Declaration) a say in major decisions affecting Hong Kong before 1997. It held to this line the whole time, through nine secret meetings and yet another parade of British officials forced to travel to Peking to petition for mercy. Again the British administration was placed in a quandary of its own making. Had the British not trumpeted the airport project so loudly, it would not have become a test for investors.

With the stakes so high, the British tried to make the Chinese see reason—as well as what their obstructionism was doing to Hong Kong's economic confidence. The result of the negotiations was a seven-point Memorandum of Understanding announced on July 4, 1991, in both London and Peking. (See appendix D.) Essentially the agreement boiled down to a Chinese green light for the project in exchange for the veto it had demanded all along. The Memorandum was immediately hailed as the Second Joint Declaration. Like the 1984 original, this one had been concluded over the heads of the Hong Kong people.

The written terms of the Memorandum have to do mostly with business. The PRC, through the state-owned Bank of China, will play a role in financing the project. The Chinese also gained a say in the awarding of contracts, a veto over any loan pushing the post-1997 airport-related debt over $640 million (HK $5 billion), and a guarantee that Britain will leave behind at least $3.2 billion (HK $25 billion) in reserves. In a nice bonus for the Chinese, Prime Minister John Major traveled to Peking to sign the agreement in September 1991, thus becoming the highest ranking Western official to visit the Chinese capital since the bloodshed on Tiananmen. In exchange for all this "the Chinese side will adopt a positive attitude to such grants, contracts and guarantees."

Although Hong Kong certainly needs an infrastructure upgrade to stay competitive, the airport matter was at bottom a question of authority. Sir David himself put it well at the outset when he said, "It is important that the Hong Kong Government remains in full and effective control of decision-taking over the affairs of Hong Kong in 1997." In short, it was now a question of British face.

The airport flap was all the more significant in that it was the first time a political development had impinged directly on the foreign business community. China's objections to the project had soured a number of potential investors. After the Memorandum was announced, some investor confidence was restored.

But although the project can now go ahead, rejoicing may be somewhat premature. Given China's desperate need for foreign currency, it is safe to predict that at least some of the airport contracts will be sent Peking's way. The business community (particularly the American business community) has to wonder whether Hong Kong will continue to be an open economy where contracts are awarded on merit, or whether it will be reduced to a Chinese province where they are allocated by politics, connections, and under-the-table contributions. It does not augur well for Hong Kong's future "autonomy" that in the first real test, what ought to have been a purely administrative matter for Hong Kong locals to decide was once again forwarded to Peking.

Rallies and Reversals

During his visit to Hong Kong in January 1990, Foreign Secretary Douglas Hurd said that the first prize for Hong Kong would be a 1997 convergence that was in accord with the wishes of Hong Kong people themselves. If this first prize could not be won, he said, second prize would be for Britain to stick to the Joint Declaration and implement democracy in Hong Kong on its own over the seven years remaining under British rule. Barely a few days later he acquiesced to an arrangement that achieved neither of the two. Instead, it has guaranteed an arrangement that accords almost completely with China's own system.

If the crisis of confidence in Hong Kong has been exacerbated since Tiananmen Square—and the government's upward revisions of its brain-drain figures suggests it has—the reason is not that Hong Kong Chinese have suddenly realized that Deng Xiaoping is not really a Chinese Thomas Jefferson. They have been well aware of that all along. What Tiananmen Square did was throw Britain's Hong Kong policies into high relief, subjecting them to a scrutiny they could not withstand. As other observers have pointed out, for the Joint Declaration to work, China had to project a modernizing and liberalizing image; Hong Kongers had to remain passive; and both sides had to gloss over the immense practical difficulties of reconciling a Western-style colony characterized by a free market and broad individual freedoms with a Marxist system that had no such experience. Above all, what was required was a gentlemen's agreement not to ask too many questions.

Such a compact could not have lasted thirteen years, much

less survive a calamitous event like Tiananmen. That brutal day only accelerated a process whose outcome was foreseen long ago: China as de facto ruler of Hong Kong even while the British flag continues to fly over Government House. Just as so many had feared, the Joint Liaison Group between the two nations has already become a quasi-government. This crisis is of British manufacture and as such has its roots as far back as 1985, when the Long Slide away from the provisions of the Joint Declaration began.

To suggest, as the government continues to do, that the brain drain and related signs of decay are without social and economic consequences courts disaster. In economic terms the downswing has begun. Although there will continue to be handsome profits to be made in Hong Kong, it today shows signs of becoming just another Chinese city, with all the corruption and uncertainty that implies. Already the papers are chronicling the breakdown of law and order in what was once one of the world's most law-abiding societies: violent crime is on the upsurge, and with it assault complaints against police.

In social terms, the lack of protection (i.e., lack of a full passport) for civil servants compromises their performance. Even if the new nationality package were to be applied exclusively to these 188,400 workers, nearly three-fourths would still find themselves unprotected. What incentive will they have to do the government's work in a way that might be good for Hong Kong but upset China? This is even more sensitive with regard to the 33,200 members of the Royal Hong Kong Police Force. (A number of officers are now suing the government, claiming they had been promised passports; should they choose to talk, their revelations could be most embarrassing.) In the past the force drew thousands of applications, but now the flow is down to a trickle; not surprisingly, the daily papers are screaming about the rising tide of lawlessness in the colony. Given all this, the remarkable thing has to be that public dissatisfaction has *not* translated into violence against the British. Not yet, at least, and one only prays.

Just how deep feelings run in Hong Kong was graphically demonstrated by the rallies held in the colony in June 1990 to commemorate the first anniversary of the bloodshed on Tiananmen Square. Estimates just before the scheduled march had it drawing no more than 30,000. The million-plus crowds of the year before were attributed to the emotion of the moment. Also keeping expectations minimal was the knowledge that Chinese representatives in the colony would be watching to see which Hong Kongers took part in any demonstration. Governor Wilson, ever mindful of Peking's interests, soberly advised that Hong Kong people would be better off "looking to the future."

As it turned out, more than 200,000 people showed up for the events, making their own long march from the Central District out to the New China News Agency offices, where the cameras that were clicking away were not always for news purposes. Tens of thousands gathered in Victoria Park for a dramatic candlelight ceremony. All Sir David could bring himself to say was that he hoped China would "understand."

5

End of Empire

IN THIS the last redoubt of imperial England, a local television station took to running a weekly series charting the Crown's often ignominious retreat from holdings that within memory spanned more than a quarter of the earth's land mass. Called "End of Empire," the series opened each week with a shot of three soldiers silhouetted against a mountain sunset, lowering the Union Jack to the strains of a dirge.

Real life is less kind. With less than six years remaining before the British quit Asia for good, such trappings as remain of Her Majesty's once proud dominion now seem like stage effects. The governor, formerly a stout expression of John Bull's self-confidence, has become a figure of jest. Foul graffiti about the Queen, the likes of which have not been seen since the Cultural Revolution, appear here and there. A visiting British foreign secretary is hooted down, and the word "colony" has been expunged from the official lexicon. Everywhere the sights and sounds of daily life hint that something has changed dramatically in a patch of China that has known little but change over its relatively brief lifespan. In Hong Kong's innumerable street markets, strains of Mandarin are increasingly heard over the Cantonese din.

The continuing brain drain, of course, remains the most inexorable indicator of local distrust of official British and Chinese promises. Whatever the well-groomed officers sitting behind their big desks inside the Hong Kong government might say, no city can continue to lose 1,200 members of its middle class each week without grave social and economic consequences. Opinion surveys show that a large number of people would like to leave; that the percentage of those actively pursuing emigration drastically increases for professionals, entrepreneurs, and managers; and that the civil servants charged with the actual running of the colony today trust neither Britain nor China.

Similar portents are noticeable in the political arena. The increasing frequency with which the governor and his minions trek to Peking is one. The growing militancy of the PRC contingent of the Joint Liaison Group in discussing matters specifically beyond its legal mandate is a signal that what negotiators feared most is now happening: that long before the last British Gurkha withdraws from the colony's defenses and the last British governor retires to the House of Lords, the scepter has been passed to China. The airport deal no doubt will only fuel further demands—just as a century and a half ago Britain responded to Chinese weakness by going back to the emperor for ever more land. With positions in government service opening up as the incumbents leave the colony, it is only a matter of time before Peking starts to move its own people into the formal power structure as well. Come 1997 the actual transfer of power will be mainly ceremonial.

In this dismal atmosphere the requirements for Hong Kong's continued survival have shifted. The practical dilemma of maintaining the same prosperous Hong Kong lifestyle and social systems with a different sovereign was magnified by a towering contradiction within the 1984 Joint Declaration. This has to do with the more or less unique structure of Hong Kong's colonial administration, whereby a centralized foreign bureaucracy, insulated from public pressure, observes liberal democratic freedoms it has in principle reserved to its own discretion. John Walden, a former colonial officer who has served on both the Executive Council and the Legislative

Council, has more than once noted that most of the rights enshrined in the Joint Declaration do not have the force of law in Hong Kong. They exist only by administrative sufferance.

Possibly no people save the English could have made such a system work. And work it has, to the extent that most people in Hong Kong have been so free that they haven't even known their real legal status. During the 1987 reform of the colony's press laws, it finally dawned on Hong Kong newspapermen that the freedoms to which they were accustomed owed themselves less to legal protection than to a pronounced British disinclination to invoke, save under extreme provocation, the vast powers the government reserves for itself. Similarly, Hong Kong's prosperity was made possible by the extension of this same distaste for intervention into the economic realm. Here the separation of spheres was fortified by the sturdy wall erected between the business community and the civil service, a wall facilitated by the difference in races between the two communities. Whatever the claims about China's "pragmatism," no one seriously believes that Peking will be anywhere near as scrupulous about such distinctions as London has been.

Consequently, if the promise in the Joint Declaration that Hong Kong's capitalist system and lifestyle shall remain unchanged is to be kept, its administrative structure must be altered to compensate for the marked tendency of the soon-to-be-overlords to stick their fingers into every pie. In short, any hopes for implementing the Joint Declaration depend on the imposition of restraints on the PRC's legal and practical ability to wield power come 1997. The final draft of the Basic Law, ratified in April 1990 by the National People's Congress in Peking, has all but killed any chance for self-restraint on China's part.

The constitutional problem of freedom vs. order is by no means a new one, though in this case it is exacerbated by the fact that the potential power-wielders are Communists, who view agreements as tactical diversions rather than strategic settlements. Two hundred years ago another former British colony saw its Founding Fathers deliberate essentially the same question, and their *Federalist Papers* remain the most incisive commentary yet produced on the difficulties of striking that delicate balance between order and liberty. Indeed, if any model exists of a one-country/two-systems arrangement, it is the United States, with its division between central and local authority. The American Constitution was a specific application of the general British understanding of limited government, and it succeeded because it vested that concept not in the "parchment promises" of legal documents but in the people themselves. It did this by holding the rulers accountable to the ruled.

In the case of Hong Kong, this would have meant enshrining in law what has long been practiced in fact, and the Joint Declaration gave a few coy winks in this direction. The provision for a legislature "constituted by elections" was a notable departure from the system prevailing in 1984, in which the Legislative Council was composed of members appointed by the governor or elected by functional constituencies (special interests such as lawyers, teachers, and laborers). The new structure would substitute democratic processes for Britain's traditional predilection against abusing its powers.

This, at least, is how members of Parliament understood the proposed arrangement when they debated the Joint Declaration in December 1984. Robert Adley noted that the swift development of democratic institutions "will make it far more difficult for the Chinese Government to interfere."[1] "We have only twelve years, and the direction of constitutional changes must be embarked on soon because Hong Kong cannot afford many mistakes," said David Heathcoat-Armory. "Other societies can afford one or two false starts, but not Hong Kong."[2]

Richard Luce, speaking for the Thatcher government as minister with special responsibility for Hong Kong, was at pains to stress the congruence between Parliament and the government on this issue. "We all fully accept that we should build up a firmly based democratic administration in Hong Kong in the years between now and 1997."[3]

These assurances, like so many others, have since flitted away in the wind, and Hong Kong increasingly appears defenseless against the assaults of 1997. The 1987 decision to put off elections until 1991—*after* China had had time to draft and approve a Basic Law—ensured, as critics predicted it would, that Hong Kong would never see the system of self-rule to which Britain and China had pledged themselves in 1984. In the wake of Tiananmen Square, after encouraging signs that the Iron Lady's spine was finally stiffening, British resolve faltered again.

This leaves two options for those concerned about the colony's future, one internal, one external. The internal option: Accountability, particularly of the civil service, must become the predominant aim of those concerned with ensuring that Hong Kong's freedoms are not surrendered along with British sovereignty. Until now the civil service has managed Hong Kong quite nicely without such controls, but until now, too, Parliament has ever been there in the background, acting as a democratic brake on potential excesses by an unaccountable colonial elite. "The accountability of the newly reformed institutions is as important as the elections themselves," argued George Robertson in the parliamentary debate in 1984. "The transition from colonial rule to a self-governing administrative region must involve open, accountable government at all levels."[4] Now that the Basic Law has stripped elections of any real meaning—only a third of the legislature will be freely elected by the people come 1997, and real power will be wielded by Peking-appointed or -approved officials— the only internal political option left is to strive to make such government as will survive more accountable. Most obviously, making a government more accountable primarily means making it more open, which in the case of Hong Kong would necessitate the passage of sunshine laws to remove the veil of secrecy that continues to cloak much of the colony's administrative life. Perhaps the new Legislative Council constituted in 1991, prodded by its first democratically elected members, will move in this direction, through governments accustomed to secrecy rarely abandon it willingly.

The great, unplayed trump card here, however, is the external option: the American card. As British influence and stature continue to wane, the United States remains the one country with enough at stake, and with enough leverage over both China and Britain, to create some insurance for Hong Kong.

American Interests

The Stars and Stripes have been in Hong Kong almost as long as the British themselves, with a consulate dating back to 1865. Yankee clippers carried opium from India to China throughout the nineteenth century, and the American merchants who brought the drug never left the infant colony so important to the trade. In her best-selling book *Hong Kong*, historian Jan Morris notes that Americans built the first church on the island (the Baptist Chapel) and financed the first 1,000-room hotel (today's Hilton, near the U.S. consulate), and that an American—one of Commodore Perry's naval officers—attended the first Christmas dinner at Government House. For a brief period in the mid-1980s, an American was even the *taipan* of Jardine Mattheson, the real-life counterpart to the fictional trading house of James Clavell's *Noble House*.

Over the years, Hong Kong has skittered in and out of the American consciousness, depending on events elsewhere in the Far East. President Franklin D. Roosevelt, naïve decolonialist that he was, brought up Hong Kong with Stalin several times, suggesting that it be internationalized. His own State Department entertained other ideas. Chiang Kai-shek, a member of the Five Powers, wanted to have Hong Kong to himself, and at least some Americans were prepared to give it to him. But when an emaciated Franklin Gimson—the former colonial secretary—emerged from years of incarceration in the Stanley concentration camp to run up the British colors after learning of the Japanese surrender, he forestalled any other designs on the colony.

After the Communist takeover of the mainland in 1949, Hong Kong became even more useful to Americans as a listening post near a China fast retreating into its age-old shell. The crushing waves of refugees that more than doubled the population of Hong Kong during the 1950s constituted a short-term burden but set off a long-term economic boom, and America was there gleaning what it could from their accounts. For their part, two generations of U.S. servicemen on leave from the Korean and Vietnamese wars have fond memories of Hong Kong and its pleasures, including the Wanchai district and the hundreds of Suzie Wongs available for a night's consolation.

Today the G.I.s have gone and Suzie Wong has moved uptown, but the indefatigable Yankee merchants have stayed. McDonald's, Burger King, and Pizza Hut are as familiar to Hong Kong children as to their U.S. counterparts in Des Moines. Local television broadcasts American shows, from "Dallas" and "Roseanne" to the Superbowl, and now even Cable News Network. Citibank is almost as prevalent a fixture as the old Hong Kong and Shanghai Bank was before it skipped off to London. The *Wall Street Journal* publishes an Asian edition out of Hong Kong. American residents of Hong Kong total just under 21,000, which makes them the largest foreign community after Filipinos (the bulk of whom are domestics). And nearly 12,000 Hong Kong students are now studying at American colleges and universities (injecting about $200 million a year into the U.S. economy).

Even more than the British, the American flag has followed trade. That the American community in Hong Kong outnumbers the British (according to some figures) is hardly surprising in view of Hong Kong's threefold allure to businessmen as a gateway to China, as a local market in itself, and as a regional center for Asia. No other city comes close. Seoul and Taipei are too far north and not nearly as sophisticated. Tokyo is too expensive and militantly provincial. Singapore is over-regulated. Bangkok has a long way to go, and Manila is simply chaos. No wonder that Hong Kong boasts the largest U.S. Chamber of Commerce outside America's borders. And of the 581 multinational corporations whose Asian operations are based in Hong Kong, America has the lion's share with 252, followed by Britain with 77.

Today the United States has an estimated $7.1 billion investment in Hong Kong, which is more than twice its investment in China and almost a quarter of all foreign investment in Hong Kong. Moreover, given Hong Kong's pivotal role in China's development (it is the largest outside investor in the mainland), the future of American investment in the PRC itself depends to a crucial degree on Hong Kong's ability to persevere in the role it has played for 150 years. The strength of the Hong Kong–China trade link came to public notice in the United States for the first time during the 1990 hearings on a proposal to revoke China's Most Favored Nation trading status, when the American Chamber of Commerce in Hong Kong sent emissaries to Capitol Hill to testify against the proposal.

The Chamber itself reveals much about American interests in Hong Kong. Founded in 1969 with 212 members, in 1990 it had about 1,100 companies and 2,800 individuals as members. American companies employ some 250,000 people in Hong Kong—10 per cent of the colony's workforce—and account for many related jobs across the border. The numbers are staggering. Hong Kongers purchased nearly $46 billion worth of American goods in 1989; that makes this tiny population America's fourteenth-largest market. The average Hong Konger buys $998 worth of U.S. goods each year, compared with $308 worth of U.S. goods for each Japanese, $265 for each South Korean, and $234 for each European.[5]

In terms of *specific* markets, Hong Kong's purchasing power rises to make-or-break dimensions. The tiny colony ranks among the top three markets worldwide for selected agricultural products, cut diamonds, and cigarettes. It is the world's largest buyer of American frozen poultry (from Mississippi), apples (from Washington), citrus fruits (from Florida), and tobacco (from North Carolina and Virginia). The United States is the colony's second-largest food supplier, just after China. More than twenty U.S. banks are licensed in Hong Kong, and each of the top ten banks in the United States maintains an office there. U.S. firms are also second among foreign insurers in Hong Kong.

Possibly the colony's greatest value to U.S. business interests is as a regional center. Among the companies that have their Asia-Pacific headquarters in Hong Kong are Bausch & Lomb, Dow Chemical, Dow Jones, Dun & Bradstreet International, Mattel, McDonnell Douglas, and Unisys. Exxon owns some 60 per cent of the utility that supplies Kowloon's electricity. Eleven states (California, Hawaii, Illinois, Iowa, Maryland, Michigan, Minnesota, New York, Ohio, Rhode Island, and Wisconsin) and thirteen ports (including Miami, San Diego, and Seattle) have set up offices in Hong Kong. Roughly half of the 5,000 new faculty to be hired for Hong Kong's universities over the next three years will be recruited from the United States.

Despite the manifest implications of this enormous American activity in Hong Kong, its value has yet to be appreciated by most Americans at home. Outside the business community, it isn't understood at all. In 1984, when Peking and London reached agreement on Hong Kong, U.S. Secretary of State

George Shultz immediately cabled his congratulations, reaffirming an American tradition of yielding to its British ally on questions concerning Hong Kong. Word went out to the U.S. consulate in Hong Kong not to say anything negative about the colony's future. In the past, when Britain and America had more or less the same interests here (and when, of course, Britain and Hong Kong shared the same interests), the position was understandable. Today, Britain's interest has diverged wildly from Hong Kong's, and therefore, by extension, from America's. In these changed circumstances, Washington's political deference to Whitehall is incomprehensible.

In the wake of Tiananmen Square, fortunately, America's traditional lack of interest in Hong Kong's political fate has begun to change, albeit at a maddeningly slow pace. Stories about Hong Kong's predicament are appearing in the U.S. press—usually countered immediately by op-ed pieces from the British diplomatic corps asserting that there are no real problems that a stiff upper lip cannot solve.

When George Bush announced in May 1990 that his administration would renew China's Most Favored Nation status, he said he made this decision in large part because "Hong Kong should not be the innocent victim of our disappointment with the Chinese administration." Contrary to some of the more enthusiastic reports in the Hong Kong press, this probably was less a determination to help Hong Kong than a convenient out for a White House that had long before decided not to impose sanctions on China but wanted a nice way around it. Nonetheless, the Bush announcement did put Hong Kong on the official list of U.S. concerns in the region, something quickly noted by the then president of the American Chamber of Commerce in Hong Kong, John Kamm. "The MFN statement was the first time Hong Kong has figured in a U.S. foreign policy decision since World War II," he says. "The fact that Hong Kong is an American outpost is only dimly perceived in Washington."

Although the Japanese have a claim of their own, Americans arguably own the largest outside investment in Hong Kong, and thus the United States, not Britain, stands to be the big loser if Hong Kong goes down the tubes. Despite this, notes Mr. Kamm, in the congressional debate on China sanctions that immediately followed the massacre at Tiananmen, Hong Kong was not mentioned once. Estimates vary, but the Hong Kong government has said that a U.S. decision to impose sanctions on the PRC would cost Hong Kong some $10 billion in business and at least 20,000 jobs. Whether or not President Bush meant what he said when he announcd the renewal of China's MFN status, he was correct when he cautioned against punishing Hong Kong for China's crimes.

For these reasons, the British understandably welcomed the American Chamber's intercession on behalf of Hong Kong during the MFN debate. At the same time, they are leery of stepped-up American interest in the colony. They realize what few will say openly: that Britain's present course of action—less a willful policy than the natural consequence of conflicting interests—undermines American interests in Hong Kong. This is by no means irrational. Today's Britain's real interest lies in getting out as quietly as possible before the whole show breaks up. By contrast, America's multi-billion-dollar investment here, and its use of the colony as a base for its Asian trade, means that U.S. interests are more closely aligned with those of the people of Hong Kong—that is, in keeping the place as free and open as it is today.

Changing U.S. Immigration Policy

Until late 1990, the United States had a restrictive immigration policy that, in contrast to those of its leading competitors, had virtually no room for business sponsorship of key immigrants who would work in U.S. firms. At a time when the United States is hoping to replace an immigration system based almost exclusively on family reunification with one based on skills, allowing U.S. corporations abroad to sponsor immigrants not only would make immigration more market-oriented but also would give American firms a competitive edge in attracting talent.

In Hong Kong the absence of such a provision has proved painful. The brain drain has meant that those left behind are more inclined to change jobs, especially if the new employer can guarantee a passport. Altogether, American firms in Hong Kong have suffered a staggering 30 per cent average annual turnover in staff. Mark Michelson, then with Business International, told me that in two years or so his small company of about fifty people had lost six employees, representing a combined experience of sixty-five years with the company. "That's the kind of people we're losing, and that's the problem everywhere," he said.

Some of this has been redressed by the Immigration Act that became law in November 1990 and has three parts aimed at Hong Kong. First was the provision allowing Hong Kong people who have been accepted for settlement in America to defer their decisions until 2002; this is a boon for Hong Kong, because it gives people an out if they need it but also an incentive to stay put. Under the previous use-it-or-lose-it-policy, recipients of U.S. visas had to relocate to the United States within four months or forfeit their visas.

Equally important was the extension of Hong Kong's overall annual quota of visas. Over the next few years this will jump from 5,000 to 10,000 per year, and later to 25,000 (the new number granted to all full-fledged countries). The word "quota" is somewhat misleading, for the figure represents the annual ceiling; actual disbursement of visas may be less, depending on the overall number of visas issued around the world. Still, this too represents a departure from the traditional U.S. approach to Hong Kong. In effect, at least for immigration purposes, Hong Kong will be treated as a nation separate from China and Britain. If this kind of treatment were extended to other areas—commercial, tax, and cultural treaties—it would re-emphasize the autonomy promised Hong Kong in the Joint Declaration.

The most revolutionary provision in the new U.S. immigration package is the one permitting American companies to sponsor targeted employees for an entry visa with a ten-year lifespan. Under this provision, American businesses with at least 100 workers in the United States and 50 overseas (they need not all be in Hong Kong) will be allowed to offer visas to employees who have at least one year's experience with the firm and work in some managerial or specialized capacity; altogether the law provides for 36,000 such visas to be distributed over the next three years.

Taken together, the three reforms mean that America will be extending some sort of insurance policy to two or three times as many Hong Kongers as Britain. Undeniably, the new law has weaknesses, and they have already been criticized in the press. The legal obligations of employers who provide visas are unclear, and certainly the potential for abuse in these uncharted waters exists. But the existence of loopholes and weaknesses is hardly surprising.

These new provisions owe their existence to the initiative of private American firms, especially Citibank, and the American Chamber of Commerce. The businessmen managed this striking feat with little or no help from organized Hong Kong human rights groups and only token assistance from the Hong Kong Economic and Trade Mission in Washington.

For instance, the genesis of the business-sponsored visas lay in a casual encounter between Citibank's Hong Kong business manager, Steve Baker, and the ranking Republican congressman on the House Immigration Committee, Hamilton Fish, who ultimately sponsored the provision. Working with other legislators—Senator Paul Simon and Representatives Steven Solarz, Bruce Morrison, and Barney Frank, to name but a few

—American businessmen helped push the Hong Kong provisions through. These same businessmen also quietly lobbied Peking on behalf of the package, and Chinese officials finally were persuaded not to object on the grounds that what would be given to the workers was not an outright passport (and the dual nationality that would imply) but an entry visa.

In the wake of this success, American energies might just as profitably be directed at reforming some of the structures that will survive 1997. One highly important change would be to open up to Americans the many consultative committees that are a crucial part of running the colony. Placing more emphasis on English as the international language would help, too: Hong Kong is the only place in Asia where English-language proficiency is actually declining. Most important of all, the civil service, 98 per cent of whose employees are local hires, needs to be internationalized.

In these as in other areas, the institutional bias against the United States continues to be an obstacle. Despite the vast U.S. commercial presence in the colony, the general commission of the Hong Kong General Chamber of Commerce has only one American member. Ira Kay, president of the trading firm Lark International and a long-time resident of the colony, confirms that even when Americans are put on key committees these are likely to be token appointments, and the Americans are often kept out of the power loop. Unfortunately, this institutional shunning continues despite an official Hong Kong government line favoring more U.S. involvement.

Instead of a say in the government, what Americans in Hong Kong are likely to get in the coming years is lucrative contracts. Already the United States has become the largest supplier to the Hong Kong government. U.S. firms, moreover, are likely to emerge on top in the bidding for the planned $16 billion infrastructure upgrades. Undoubtedly, some American companies stand to reap small fortunes in the short term from such projects.

Without structural political reform, however, American business will in the long run find its opportunities in Hong Kong shrinking with everyone else's. So long as the British government and the governor of Hong Kong persist in kow-towing to Peking, confidence will not be recovered, and the potential for violence will escalate. The American business community recognizes that rising crime and falling GDP rates are no accident. In October 1988, the American Chamber of Commerce lobbied Peking for stronger human rights guarantees for post-1997 Hong Kong. Although American executives still prefer to go around the British rather than air disagreements publicly, the American business community has done more than other segment of the Hong Kong population to harden Hong Kong's softening foundations. For this it has received little or no credit.

Needed: A Lobby in Washington

What is surprising, at least from an American perspective, is that despite these considerable American interests and the clear progress that has been made in Washington, Hong Kong has no real spokesman in the nation that, next to China itself, has the greatest stake in its future. There is an economic mission in Washington, led by the able Peter Lo, and it does a splendid job on trade issues. But Hong Kong's crisis is political, and on this all-important front only two voices are raised in the United States: Britain's and China's. In the crucial run-up to 1997, each of these two colonial powers reserves for itself the right to speak for the people of Hong Kong.

This arrangement reflects poorly on the Hong Kong community, especially the would-be reformers. Because not one of Hong Kong's new political parties has sent a representative to make its case in Washington, American perceptions of Hong Kong's crisis are decidedly skewed. They derive largely from annual visits to the United States by a Hong Kong governor who emphasizes the need to "trust" China and who reassures China that no real measure of Hong Kong autonomy will ever get past him. On Capitol Hill, Hong Kong's image is further eroded by its own mission. When I asked its chief for an example of something he lobbied for solely in Hong Kong's interests, not China's or Britain's, he cited only his efforts to get Congress to acquiesce in the forced return of Vietnamese —hardly a helpful kind of p.r. when America is being asked to open its doors to the Hong Kong Chinese. Indeed, it's interesting that forced repatriation of boat people is the *only* political issue the trade mission involves itself with; this contributes to the general impression that the Hong Kong people are responsible for the forced returns when in fact the policy is, like everything else, made in London and imposed on the colony without regard to its opinions. But if the American people have a false image of Hong Kong, Hong Kong people have only themselves to blame for allowing the governments of Peking and London to act on their behalf unchallenged.

The more's the pity, because there are considerable avenues of action open. "In American politics," says S. B. Woo, "there are three ways to exert influence: through elections, with appointments, or as a lobby. Of these three, lobbies are the most effective, because they can exert influence on a larger range of people." Mr. Woo's opinion merits attention, because as lieutenant governor of Delaware he was the highest-ranking Chinese-American in U.S. politics.

In the absence of an accountable Hong Kong lobby that could direct attention toward nuts-and-bolts issues, American interest in Hong Kong tends to be sporadic and focused on highly visible but generally vague resolutions on human rights, or on calls for unrealistic increases in immigration quotas. This helps no one.

The real battle in getting the last immigration bill passed was in crafting a definition of a skilled worker congruent with U.S. law and applicable to Hong Kong. Even with general agreement that entry into the United States ought to be based more on having a marketable skill than on having a sister in Pittsburgh, there was little consensus on what constitutes a "skill." In fact, in a book advocating a more skills-based immigration criterion, economist George Borjas conceded that the point systems adopted by, for instance, Canada and Australia are highly imprecise.

Most point systems established by governments will inevitably confuse education with skills and be prejudiced accordingly. "In the United States people think of a skilled person as someone with a college degree," says Citibank's Eddie Ng. "But in Hong Kong the real skills people have to offer are experience." John Watkins of Northwest Airlines concurs. "The one misconception we run into is always education levels of Hong Kong people relative to those in the United States," he says. "There is not the opportunity here to go to college that there is in America, but I have a lot of people who have the personal knowledge, skills, and experience that an MBA graduate will not acquire for years."

In lobbying for the bill, members of the business community met the issue head-on. Originally they had hoped to push through some kind of protection for *all* their employees, but Congress would consider only managers and those with special skills. This was where education became a problem, inasmuch as terms such as "manager" and "executive" are defined by regulation, not by statute, and one of the criteria used is possession of a college degree. To get around this difficulty, in drafting the language of the law the businessmen were careful to take the terms from existing regulations: the term "officer," for example, was taken from the Delaware Corporate Code (most American companies are incorporated in this state) and the term "supervisor" from the National Labor Relations Act. In so doing they subtly shifted the emphasis of U.S. criteria from education to experience.

Even with this law in place, a number of side approaches

remain unexplored. E-2 visas, to name but one, do not confer the privilege of citizenship but have nearly the same effect; recipients can remain in the United States as long as they like, and any children born during their stay (as well as anyone who marries an American) are eligible for full passports. No minimum amount of money is specified—the law states only that the investment must be "substantial"—but lawyers say it may be as low as $100,000. These visas come under a special bilateral treaty between Washington and London, which currently applies only to those British with the right of abode in Britain. There is, however, no reason why this category of visas could not be broadened to include those from British dependent territories. "All this would take is an administrative ruling by the State Department," says immigration attorney Paul Shearman Allen. "This could open the way for 300,000 or so people from Hong Kong."

On a broader scale, the new U.S.–Hong Kong Policy Act introduced in late 1991 by Senator Mitch McConnell (R.-Ky.) would go a long way toward boosting confidence. Essentially the bill does no more than reaffirm the terms of the 1984 Joint Declaration, particularly in regard to Hong Kong's promised autonomy. But by putting the United States on record, it means American policymakers will be bound to insist on that autonomy in appropriate international forums— at least in such areas as landing rights, immigration, and trade. For the gravest danger Hong Kong faces from America is that of being lumped together with China. "What if some day a U.S. congressman stands up and asks, 'Why do we have one textile quota for China and one for Hong Kong?' " asks United Democrats chairman Martin Lee. "Hong Kong doesn't discriminate against *any* American products—we have the most open economy in the world—yet where this is not clearly understood we fear we may be punished for China's deeds."

For this reason the United States might profitably use the McConnell bill as a springboard for a free-trade arrangement

(FTA) with Hong Kong. From Hong Kong's point of view this would require no sacrifices, because, as Mr. Lee points out, Hong Kong already practices free trade with the United States; an FTA, however, would guarantee its continued access to the U.S. market after 1997 free of China's mischief (such as the use of prison labor, discriminatory trade practices, and human rights violations). From America's point of view, an FTA with Hong Kong, pursued at the same time Washington is about to clinch such an arrangement with Mexico, would help ensure that American business keeps its access in Asia, as well as guard against the formation of a regional economic bloc around protectionist Japan. Even if there were no political crisis over Hong Kong, the economic advantages of such a pact would be compelling.

Looking Toward the Sunset

Let us be clear: the United States cannot "save" Hong Kong. So long as Britain remains determined to see the colony handed over in 1997 bound hand and foot, any outside power is limited in its influence. But the United States can do two things. First, if the colony is destined to lose its freedoms once the PRC resumes sovereignty, America can offer multitudes of hard-working and talented Hong Kongers shelter within its own borders, where they would undoubtedly become but the latest wave of people to wash up on America's shores only to transform their desperation into increased opportunity for all. On a more limited scale, the insurance policies that American firms in Hong Kong can extend to their employees in the interim will help brace a colony lashed from all directions.

By making the case for the freedoms that allow Hong Kong to prosper today, the United States can increase its chances tomorrow. Whether this takes the form of internationalizing the civil service, reversing the decline in English standards, or impressing upon Peking the commercial imperatives of preserving Hong Kong's tradition of common law, Americans ought to be ready to lead. None of these measures will preserve the Hong Kong of the past. But together they might help conserve some of its soul against the day when it may once again be permitted to live in freedom.

Epilogue

IN EARLIER days Europeans doing business in Hong Kong found it necessary to create a position, called *comprador*, for a Chinese who would serve as an intermediary to all Chinese employees and Chinese officials. The *comprador* had wide latitude, for all the European company cared about was whether the assigned task had been completed. A century and a half after the Union Jack was set on Hong Kong soil, Sir David Wilson has himself become a kind of *comprador* to Deng Xiaoping, charged with coming up with the right mix of rationalizations to explain why Britain is doing precisely what China asks, whether packing off refugees to Hanoi or prosecuting democrats with bullhorns.

And so as the sun begins to set on the British Empire, we are evidently not going to be spared the full spectacle. Where once Chinese emperors trembled in their palaces at the thought of England's wrath, Chairman Mao's heirs amuse themselves by putting Britain's governor through the full kowtow. The Mother of Parliaments becomes the incongruous setting for thunderous speeches by one Right Honorable Member after another on the menace of representative government. And the most fiercely anti-Communist prime minister in Britain's history sets the tone by replacing Chamberlain's "peace in our time" with "prosperity in our time"—making sure, all the while, that Britain's back door remains firmly latched against any Hong Kong Chinese fool enough to disagree—all to the cheers of big business, unelected local legislators, foreign rulers, and innumerable others busy angling for future favor.

Sadly, what all this makes clear is that Hong Kong's only real hope lies with China itself. The question today is whether the Celestial Empire follows the path of Eastern Europe and the Soviet Union or whether its aging politburo responds to the popular thirst for greater freedom with ever more draconian countermeasures. In the meantime, in that grey chasm between things hoped for and things possible, Britain still holds the key, legally, politically, morally. If Hong Kong is not to collapse even before the red star is run up the flagpole over Government House, if it is not to succumb to the hanging cloud of despair, then Britain needs to assert its control in the waning years of power. On the evidence thus far this seems most unlikely.

Oddly enough, the failure to do so is inviting precisely the specter of an ungovernable colony such acquiescence was meant to avoid. Such signs as there are point ominously to frustration ripening ultimately into violence. The one-year commemorations of Tiananmen in Hong Kong were noteworthy not only for attracting crowds ten times larger than anyone had predicted but also for the range of people they drew. Over two days of remarkable observances, including a moving candlelight ceremony at Victoria Park, I observed not a single English-language sign. The atmosphere was suffused with an overriding sense of Chinese nationalism, confused, divided, and latent though it may be.

What direction this nationalism will take is anyone's guess. Something of a schizophrenia hovers over the Hong Kong Chinese, who take pride in their Chineseness but understand that a certain something else distinguishes them from their brothers and sisters on the mainland. It is not, of course, without its uglier side: the hostility toward the Vietnamese boat people (one *South China Morning Post* survey said most

Hong Kongers would rather let them drown than land) is indefensible, as well as counterproductive at a time when the colony is courting world sympathies. But it is also unremarkable in light of the Hong Kong government's incessant propaganda on the subject. Whether this is deliberate on the part of the government or not, the boat people serve the government's interest both by distracting Hong Kongers from their own problems and by reducing outside sympathy (hence outside pressure to act). The astute observer will notice that while this is a British decision, authorities make sure that the faces of the policemen forcing Vietnamese back on the planes are all Hong Kong Chinese.

Within Hong Kong, the great unspoken worry is what happens when the bulk of this populace finally face the fact that they are stuck, and when that realization is combined with some incident that sets off age-old feelings of Chinese xenophobia. It might be ignited by a whisper, say, that Britain was stripping the place of all value before it pulled out; recall that the last riots were set off by a fare increase at the Star Ferry. Given the sizable number of people who already believe that Britain skims from the treasury (it doesn't, of course, but the secrecy of the figures only fuels suspicions), any such slight already possesses a built-in credibility. Colonial governments on their way out are not the most popular.

Adding to the unease of those who worry about the potential for chaos is the indeterminate state of the police. In the last riots to afflict Hong Kong, the paramount credit for containing the situation went to the Royal Hong Kong Police, whose members, particularly the ethnic Chinese, displayed immense fortitude in the face of threats and mob violence. The difference is that back then security officers had the assurance of knowing that at the end of the day Britain would still be in power. Today the policemen know that China will be taking over, and that their service on behalf of the Crown has already tainted them in party minds. Small wonder that applications to the force have dwindled to the point where the police are actually closing some stations. With these kinds of pressures, and with their families possibly imperiled, in the event of massive unrest can these policemen be expected to risk their necks on behalf of a departing power—an ungrateful one at that?

If you go down to the Hong Kong information offices in the old French mission and ask the kind gentleman there, he will undoubtedly answer that the colony has been buffeted by strong winds before and has survived. Nationalist uprisings on the mainland led to a general strike in 1925; the Japanese invaded and occupied Hong Kong during the Second World War; during the early 1950s more than a million and a half refugees poured in from across the border in the wake of the Communist takeover; a U.N.-sponsored embargo on China trade during the Korean War took away the colony's largest markets; and in 1967 the Cultural Revolution spilled over into anarchy on Hong Kong's usually well-ordered streets. Besides, he might add (as the governor usually does), whatever China's record at home, it has always adhered to international agreements.

But there's the rub, isn't it, for China considers Hong Kong an internal matter—how does the Joint Declaration put it?—an accident "left over from history." Indeed, China has always considered Hong Kong thus, and only British resolve has kept the colony afloat these many years. Today that resolve has gone, the flag will soon follow, and all of Hong Kong's riches cannot save it from its fate. Although generations of British civil servants have administered the colony brilliantly and without political rancor, the price of this paternalistic competence was to leave their charges singularly unprepared for the gravest challenge of their lives, the transition to Peking rule. Not least among Hong Kong's problems throughout this mess has been that those deciding Hong Kong's future are not those who have to live with it. Having arrived in a cloud of opium, Her Majesty's representatives are sidling out under the cover of contract.

Anyone who has known Hong Kong as a home, as I was privileged to do, knows well that the human costs behind this tragedy never quite make it to the front page. The wife of a prominent Hong Kong attorney tells me all their friends have emigrated; they wonder what country their son will grow up in. A secretary who moved to Canada tells me about a sister in Los Angeles and a brother in Sydney. A pregnant former colleague stays with me in Washington for three months so that her child will have a U.S. passport. These are the lucky ones, the people with options. A century ago, Emerson coldly observed that the Empire was "more just than kind"; today, here, it is neither.

Indeed, at a time when the rest of the world is busy shucking off its Communist overlords, capitalist Hong Kong finds itself pushed hard in the opposite direction. China is not Poland, of course, nor is it the Soviet Union; it is still hard to believe that the present totalitarian system can long prevail against the clear wishes of more than a billion citizens who have watched freedom break out all over the rest of the earth. If Peking's creaking gerontocracy appears to overreact to indigenous Hong Kong political leaders, it is because these old men know in their bones that what distinguishes a Boris Yeltsin from an Andrei Sakharov, a Lech Walesa from a Father Popieluszko, or a Martin Lee from a Fang Lizhi is an institutional political base whose mere existence embarrasses the totalitarian claim. And if the day comes when China looks to reconstitute itself as a civilized state, these nascent Hong Kong leaders will find themselves resurrecting a nation where once they had hoped only to save a city.

Already these leaders are exerting a powerful appeal in Hong Kong. The September 1991 elections for the Legislative Council swept the democratic candidates into office and confirmed Martin Lee as the most popular political figure in the colony. This is precisely Peking's nightmare, a genuine man of the people. But it also puts Britain in a bind. Give in to Lee's demand that the appointed members of the Executive and Legislative councils reflect the manifest will of the people, and the Hong Kong government risks more trouble from China. Resist, and it faces potentially explosive discontent at home. In short, at a time when the Hong Kong government's challenges are escalating daily, its authority is diminishing. In every area of disagreement Martin Lee may now challenge those running the colony with the haunting question, "Who elected you?"

For the Chinese and British both, the twilight of empire is proving an ironic denouement. What the British achieved in Hong Kong could be said to reflect a Chinese ideal. The veteran Chinese journalist Tsang Ki-fan put it this way just before he died in 1988: "This is the only Chinese society that, for a brief span of 100 years, lived through an ideal never realized at any time in the history of Chinese societies—a time when no man had to live in fear of the midnight knock on the door." How sad to see it all sacrificed at the precise moment when history has vindicated the experiment.

Impact of the Brain Drain on Hong Kong's Economy

Report by the U.S. Consulate General in Hong Kong, October 1989

The following is an excerpt from a report released by the U.S. Consulate in Hong Kong and subsequently published in the magazine of the American Chamber of Commerce in Hong Kong. Its release dismayed Hong Kong government officials, not so much because of its content—most of what it said was already well known—but because the U.S. government was acknowledging the brain drain. This itself was controversial in that the consulate staff were under instructions not to say anything negative about the situation in Hong Kong.

EXECUTIVE SUMMARY   A recently released Hong Kong Government study concluded that overall emigration is increasing and that a considerable portion of it represents an outflow of scarce talents, the so-called brain drain. The economic consequences of this outflow are already being felt and will become increasingly evident in the next several years. The private sector is considering a number of responses, but the likely outcome in the 90s is higher costs and possibly reduced operating efficiency. The government intends to increase spending on tertiary education and has announced plans to ease immigration rules and to provide for a management training scheme. It will also seek to improve the quality of life here so as to attract returnees. While the brain drain's effects will be mitigated somewhat by the existence of a pool of hardworking and ambitious workers, the phenomenon may adversely affect Hong Kong's relative attractiveness as a regional financial and services center in the 1990s.

Study Outlines Emigration Pattern

A recent Hong Kong Government (HKG) study examined the dimensions of the "brain drain" problem. According to the HKG, emigrants (including all family members) totaled 45,800 in 1988, and 42,000 are projected to depart in 1989. While emigration is not a new phenomenon here by any means, these figures stand in stark contrast to the average of 20,000 per year in the early 1980s. Projected outflow ranges from 50,000 to 60,000 per year in the 90s, and it is widely predicted that the high side of this range will be reached in 1990/92 as a result of June 4 [the Tiananmen Square crackdown].

Half million to depart by 1997. Immigration policies as to intake levels and profile of desired immigrants of destination countries such as Canada, Australia, and the United States are critical factors in this projection. Even if we assume the lower figure for 1990–1996, the HKG report implies that almost 500,000, or 8 percent of Hong Kong's current population, will have departed in the decade prior to 1997.

Brain Drain Phenomenon

Set against the backdrop of an extremely tight labor market (the unemployment rate recently dropped to 1.2 percent), the term "brain drain" was used as early as 1987 to refer to net outflow of key personnel in the managerial, technical, and professional areas. Earlier surveys had established that as many as half of the Hong Kong Chinese in these occupational categories were planning to leave in order to obtain a foreign passport or already had a family member in possession of such. The recent government study confirms this predilection as it concludes that fully 25 percent of all emigrants or 7,400 were in the "professional, technical, administrative, and managerial" occupational category in 1987. In 1988, 11,200 emigrants fell into the same category and accounted for an identical percentage of the total.

According to the government report, 300,000 people were listed in this category in Hong Kong in 1988, implying that the pool of such workers shrank by almost 4 percent due to emigration. Using a narrower definition of top workers for a total of only 220,000, former Institute of Personnel Management (IPM is a local private professional body of personnel managers) research director Paul Kirkbridge estimates that shrinkage is closer to 5 percent a year. Allowing for a repatriation rate of 20 percent as quoted by HKG sources, net outflow due to emigration amounted to 3 to 4 percent of the total pool per year. However, the net outflow rate may be higher for certain occupations. For example, the experience of one major U.S. bank here is that the repatriation rate averages only some 5 to 10 percent, implying a proportionately higher rate of net outflow.

Exact statistics on sectoral impact are not available (IPM has undertaken an extensive study whose results will be made public in the near future). However, effects on local business are exacerbated by the fact that émigré talents are concentrated in certain key areas based on foreign demand and immigration policy. Thus, academics and computer and financial services professionals have been among the most actively courted talents. An ongoing study of financial sector firms concludes that turnover among middle to top managers has risen from about 12 percent in 1986 to an unacceptably high 30 percent for the last two years running. In one major U.S. bank's experience, such rates have been encountered elsewhere only in crisis situations. The impact of the drain is magnified by the fact that Hong Kong's economy is more and more driven by the provision of specialized financial and business services on a regional basis and that the talent drain may be concentrated in precisely those occupations for which demand is growing the fastest.

ECONOMIC CONSEQUENCES

There is every reason to believe that this drain will continue unless confidence in the territory's political future takes a dramatic upturn. Indeed, Hong Kong governor Sir David Wilson gave pride of place to this issue in his annual address to the Legislative Council this year. This was in contrast to no mention in the 1987 address and less prominence in the 1988 message. One set of proposals made by the governor had to do with upgrading the educational system and enhancing the quality of life here to attract returnees. But if events and government policy are unable to moderate the outflow, current trends provide a guide to the economic consequences for Hong Kong. These outcomes and their implied effects were summarized in a November 1988 study commissioned by Peat Marwick management consultants in Hong Kong:

• Loss of highly skilled and experienced middle managers/ professional (reduced efficiency, use of less qualified in key positions).

• Higher labor turnover at all levels (from less than 1 percent in 1982 to over 5 percent in 1987; increase in "job hopping").

• Higher compensation packages (contributing to inflationary spiral).

• Growth of service sector/lower investment by multinationals (service-sector investment by multinationals discouraged; some operations transferred elsewhere in the region).

• Loss of accountability (decline in employee loyalty, difficult to assign responsibility for decisions).

• Social consequences (loss of community leaders).

• Capital outflow (family and asset "portfolio diversification" leads to lower level of investment and domestic business activity).

[The report went on to deal with "Private Sector Responses" and "Public Policy Responses." The following paragraphs concluded the report.]

HKG aims to attract returnees but prospects mixed. In his 1988 address, the governor made mention of the need to provide more international schools to meet the demands of future returnees. Going a step further in his 1989 speech, he introduced a new subsidy scheme to encourage the development of private education and also spoke of the need to improve Hong Kong's physical environment. Both measures are in part aimed at enhancing the attractiveness of the territory for potential returnees. However, the results of an unpublished IPM poll of almost 300 returnees give little cause for comfort. Fully 60 percent said that they would definitely or probably depart Hong Kong prior to 1997, and virtually all reported that their main motive in returning was financial.

Given a goal of income maximization subject to a time constraint, such returnees can be expected to contribute to a higher rate of job turnover and, as a result, to some of the problems identified by the Peat Marwick research report.

"Astronauts" live in two worlds. Further evidence of the impermanence of many of these workers is the new class of "astronaut" managers who return to Hong Kong after dropping their families in the country which has granted them residence. Forced to maintain a peripatetic existence divided between their families resident in Canada or Australia and lucrative careers in Hong Kong, the "astronauts" may also walk a fine line between legitimate travel to the territory and physical residency requirements of their adopted homes.

Grads return only after failing in job search abroad. The HKG has already spent considerable sums on research and advertising in order to lure back Hong Kong Chinese graduates of U.S. universities, but the effort has met with disappointing results thus far. Most such returnees report that they decided to return only after failing to find suitable employment in the U.S. job market.

Current Events in China

Policy Statement by the British
Foreign Secretary, June 6, 1989

On the day after the Tiananmen Square crackdown, Sir Geoffrey Howe spoke in the House of Commons on events in China and their implications for Hong Kong:

DURING THE LAST FEW DAYS, units of the Chinese Army have been engaged in the violent suppression of peaceful and popular demonstrations in the streets of Peking. The indiscriminate and unprovoked use of military force has caused the death or injury of thousands of students and other innocent civilians. I am sure that all members of the House will share that sense of horror and join in the international condemnation of the slaughter of innocent people.

I summoned the Chinese Chargé d'Affaires yesterday. I told him that the British Government and people were united in condemning the merciless treatment of peaceful demonstrators, and deeply deplored the use of force to suppress the democratic aspirations of the Chinese people.

I told him that the British Government looked to the Chinese authorities to fulfil their obligations to Hong Kong in the Joint Declaration of 1984.

I reminded him of the responsibilities of the Chinese Government to ensure the safety of British citizens and Hong Kong residents. I expressed concern at the maltreatment of British journalists, particularly Michael Fathers of *The Independent* and Jonathan Mirksey of *The Observer*. We have since seen disturbing reports of the ill treatment of Kate Adie of the BBC.

Our Ambassador in Peking and his staff have been working round the clock to ensure the safety of British citizens and Hong Kong residents in Peking and, as far as possible, in other parts of China. The Embassy have advised against travel to any part of China. They have also advised those who are concerned about their safety and have no pressing need to remain in China to leave immediately.

Since the Cultural Revolution, there has been a substantial improvement in relations between the United Kingdom and the People's Republic of China as the Chinese Government has sought to broaden its contacts with the international community and to introduce economic and other reforms. Friends of China in this House and around the world must share the hope that sane and balanced government will be swiftly and securely restored in Peking. In present circumstances, however, there can be no question of continuing normal business with the Chinese authorities.

Her Majesty's Government have, therefore, decided on the following action:

• All scheduled ministerial exchanges between Britain and China have been suspended. The visit of the Chinese Minister of Justice, who was due to arrive here tomorrow, has been canceled. My Right Honourable Friend, the Minister of Agriculture, Fisheries and Food, has also canceled his forthcoming visit to China.

• The proposed visit of Their Royal Highnesses The Prince and Princess of Wales to China in November clearly cannot take place so long as those responsible for the atrocities over the past weekend remain in control of the Chinese Government.

• All high-level military contacts with China have been suspended.

• All arms sales to China have been banned.

At the same time, the Government are examining how we can respond to any requests for humanitarian assistance from nongovernmental organizations.

The whole House will share the Government's special concern about the implications for Hong Kong of what has been happening in Peking. The Government understand and share the grave concern felt by the people of Hong Kong. We have all been deeply impressed by the strength and restraint of their response to what has happened.

Everything that has been accomplished in Hong Kong has been achieved in the unique context of the geography and history of the Territory, and by the talent and enterprise of its people. All that underlines the extent to which the future prosperity of Hong Kong must depend upon a successful and secure partnership with the government and people of China. That objective is enshrined in the commitments made by the British Government and the Government of China under the Joint Declaration.

Those commitments were reaffirmed by the Chargé d'Affaires when he called on me yesterday. But it is self-evident that if we are to have confidence in the commitment of the Chinese Government to their obligations, there must be a stable and responsible government in Peking. The British Government will stand by its obligations under the Joint Declaration. The Government and the House look to the Government of the People's Republic of China to live up to that international commitment as well.

The events in Peking must affect the prospects and procedure for implementation of the Joint Declaration. Consultations about the second draft of the Basic Law for Hong Kong have been suspended. It is also difficult to see how our contacts with the Chinese Government about the future of Hong Kong can continue in present circumstances.

Meanwhile, I can assure the House that we shall be conducting a thorough examination of the programme for advancing and consolidating effective democracy in Hong Kong. We are considering urgently what further steps can be taken to enshrine and protect Hong Kong's freedoms and way of life after 1997.

All of us in this House are acutely conscious of the wish of the people of Hong Kong to secure some form of assurance for themselves and their families. I know that this has been one of the issues studied by the Select Committee on Foreign Affairs. Some commentators have recommended that a right of abode in this country should be given to the 3¼ million people in Hong Kong who hold British nationality. We share the desire of the House to do everything we can to enhance the security of the people of Hong Kong. On that basis, the Government are looking urgently and sympathetically at the scope for flexibility. But the House will appreciate the reason why we could not easily contemplate a massive new immigration commitment which could more than double the ethnic minority population of the United Kingdom—a possibility that cannot be disregarded. Our overriding aim must be to do everything possible to secure the continuation of those conditions in Hong Kong that have led to its outstanding success over the last century.

I hope the House will send a message to the people of Hong Kong, reaffirming our commitment to their secure, stable, and prosperous future.

The Chinese people are seeking from their Communist leadership rights and liberties which are taken for granted in the free world. The slaughter in Peking is a tragic setback to the campaign for democracy, but I hope this House will send a united message.

China cannot ignore the lessons which are being learned elsewhere in the World. Economic prosperity and personal liberty go hand in hand. People will not forever tolerate government by repression.

Hong Kong feelings were well expressed in a series of ads that ran in local papers after Tiananmen. This one appeared in the South China Morning Post *on July 5, 1989.*

There's no point in being almost British

She went to school in Britain.

She conducts her business in English.

She remembers standing with thousands in Kowloon to catch a glimpse of the Queen.

She doesn't think about freedom because she takes it for granted.

She is a British subject in a British colony.

She is one of the millions of people for whom Hong Kong is home. People who would be an asset to any community. But who want to continue living here.

All they want is some form of insurance for the future. And the only form of insurance that will mean anything to them is the right of abode in Britain.

Otherwise, being almost British is like being homeless.

APPENDIX D

Memorandum of Understanding: The New Airport in Hong Kong

Agreement Between Britain and China, June 1991

AFTER FRIENDLY DISCUSSIONS in Beijing between representatives of the Government of the United Kingdom of Great Britain and Northern Ireland and representatives of the Government of the People's Republic of China from 27–30 June 1991, the two Governments, bearing in mind

- the urgent need for a new airport in Hong Kong in order to ensure and develop its prosperity and stability,
- the need for the airport project to be cost-effective and not to impose a financial burden on the Government of the Hong Kong Special Administrative Region of the People's Republic of China after 30 June 1997, and
- the need for practical and workable arrangements to allow work connected with the new airport to be carried out speedily and efficiently,

have reached the following understandings:

A. Between now and 30 June 1997 the Hong Kong Government will complete the Airport Core Programme projects listed in the Annex to this Memorandum of Understanding to the maximum extent possible. The Hong Kong Government will be responsible for the construction of projects covered by this Memorandum up to 30 June 1997.

B. The Chinese Government will support the construction of the new airport and related projects. It will indicate clearly to interested potential investors in accordance with the principles enshrined in this Memorandum that obligations related to the airport projects entered into or guaranteed by the Hong Kong Government will

147

continue to be valid and be recognised and protected by the Hong Kong Special Administrative Region Government from 1 July 1997. The Chinese Government have accepted that the Bank of China will play an appropriate part, for example in the syndication of loans for the airport projects, and that Chinese construction firms may compete in the normal way for projects connected with the airport.

C. On important matters relating to the airport project that straddle 30 June 1997, the Chinese and British Governments will carry out consultations in a spirit of cooperation and in accordance with the Sino-British Joint Declaration. An Airport Committee will be constituted for this purpose under the auspices of the Sino-British Joint Liaison Group, with membership drawn equally from both sides. Its tasks will be as follows:

(i) The British side will consult the Chinese side within the Airport Committee before the Hong Kong Government grants major airport-related franchises or contracts straddling 30 June 1997 or guarantees airport-related debt straddling 30 June 1997. The Chinese side will adopt a positive attitude to such grants, contracts, and guarantees. Up to one month after the British side provide details of the proposals will be allowed for discussion between the two sides in each case. The governing criteria in the case of a decision on a franchise will be the profitability and efficiency of that franchise;

(ii) The British side will consult the Chinese side within the Airport Committee before the Hong Kong Government proceeds with any major airport project other than those in the Annex to this Memorandum and any of the current Airport Core Programme projects in the Annex for which the bulk of government expenditure will fall after 30 June 1997. Such projects will only be initiated if the two sides have reached a common view concerning them.

D. The Chinese Government will adopt a positive attitude to necessary and reasonable borrowing by the Hong Kong Government to be repaid after 30 June 1997. If the total amount of debt to be repaid after 30 June 1997 will not exceed HK Dollars 5 billion [7.8 Hong Kong dollars = 1 U.S. dollar], the Hong Kong Government will be free to borrow as necessary while informing the Chinese Government. If the total amount of such debt will exceed HK Dollars 5 billion, such borrowing will only proceed if a common view has been reached concerning the proposal.

E. On the basis of the above understanding the Hong Kong Government will plan its finances with the firm objective that the fiscal reserves on 30 June 1997 to be left for the use of the Hong Kong Government will not be less than HK Dollars 25 billion.

F. In order to facilitate the construction of the new airport in Hong Kong there will be established an Airport Authority and a Consultative Committee.

(i) The Airport Authority Ordinance will be modelled as far as possible on the Mass Transit Railway Corporation Ordinance. The Hong Kong Government will retain power to direct the Authority and responsibility for key areas of policy up to 30 June 1997. The Hong Kong Government will be willing to consider and take into account views of the Chinese side when the Hong Kong Government is drawing up the draft Bill on the Authority.

(ii) The Hong Kong Government is willing to appoint a Hong Kong based individual from the Bank of China Group to sit as a full member on the board of the Airport Authority. This member will have equal right with the other members. The Chinese side will no doubt give the Hong Kong Government some suggestions as to who this member should be.

(iii) The Hong Kong Government will set up a Consultative Committee on the new airport and related projects. The Committee may discuss any relevant matter but will have no decision-making power. It should not delay the progress of the projects.

(iv) The Hong Kong Government will inform the Chinese side of the members of the Airport Authority and Consultative Committee whom it is proposed to appoint, and will be willing to listen to any views that the Chinese side might have, before deciding on the appointments. The Hong Kong Government is willing to consider the appointment of a vice-Chairman of the Airport Authority about two years after its establishment.

G. Both Governments wish to intensify consultation and cooperation over Hong Kong issues in the approach to 30 June 1997. As part of this intensified consultation, the British Foreign Secretary and the Chinese Minister for Foreign Affairs will meet twice a year to discuss matters of mutual concern, and the Director of the Hong Kong and Macau Office under the State Council and the Governor of Hong Kong will also hold regular meetings.

This Memorandum of Understanding will come into operation on signature by Heads of Government.

The foregoing record represents the understanding reached between the Government of the United Kingdom of Great Britain and Northern Ireland and the Government of the People's Republic of China upon the matters referred to therein.

ANNEX

Airport Core Programme Projects: The Airport (first runway and associated facilities) / North Lantau Expressway / West Kowloon Reclamation / West Kowloon Expressway / Western Harbour Crossing / Route 3 (part) / Airport Railway / That part of the Central and Wanchai Reclamation that relates to the Airport Railway / Lantau Fixed Crossing (including rail portion and Route 3 interchange) / Tung Chung Development Phase I.

Notes

CHAPTER ONE

1. Jan Morris, *Hong Kong* (New York: Viking Press, 1989), p. 72.
2. J. L. Cranmer-Byng, ed., *An Embassy to China: Lord Macartney's Journal 1793–94* (London, 1962), p. 340. Quoted in Jonathan Spence, *The Search for Modern China* (New York: Norton, 1990), p. 123.
3. G. B. Endacott, *A Short History of Hong Kong* (Hong Kong: Oxford University Press, 1964), p. 10.
4. Kevin Rafferty, *City on the Rocks* (London: Viking Press, 1989), p. 114.
5. Endacott, *A Short History of Hong Kong*, p. 18.
6. Rafferty, *City on the Rocks*, p. 116.
7. *Hong Kong Annual Report 1957* (Hong Kong: Government Information Services, 1957), p. 13.
8. *Hong Kong Annual Report 1960* (Hong Kong: Government Information Services, 1960), p. 15.

CHAPTER TWO

1. Joint Statement of the British and Chinese Governments, in Joseph Y. S. Cheng, *Hong Kong: In Search of a Future* (Hong Kong: Oxford University Press, 1984), p. 248.
2. Ironically, China's fidelity to international agreements has now become the cornerstone of the British government's case. The governor, Sir David Wilson, suggested in an address to Washington's National Press Club on October 16, 1989, that "China has an extremely good reputation for sticking to its international agreements and I think it's a reputation second to none."
3. T. L. Tsim, *South China Morning Post*, May 7, 1978.
4. Peter Wesley-Smith, "Hong Kong and 1997: The Options," address to the Rotary Club of Hong Kong, February 16, 1982.
5. Felix Patrikeeff, *Mouldering Pearl* (London: George Philip, 1989), p. 120.
6. David Bonavia, *Hong Kong 1997: The Final Settlement* (Hong Kong: South China Morning Post, 1985), p. 106.
7. Ibid., p. 107.

8. Ibid.

9. Great Britain, *Hansard's Parliamentary Debates* (Commons), October 31, 1983, p. 725.

10. Bonavia, *Hong Kong 1997*, p. 117.

11. "China's Town," *Asian Wall Street Journal*, July 10, 1990.

12. Kevin Rafferty, *City on the Rocks* (London: Viking Press, 1989), p. 419.

13. Ibid., p. 420.

14. Bonavia, *Hong Kong 1997*, p. 119.

15. Patrikeeff, *Mouldering Pearl*, p. 136.

Chapter Three

1. Derek Davies, "Dark Voices Prophesying Gloom," *Far Eastern Economic Review*, October 11, 1984, p. 41.

2. Great Britain, *Hansard's Parliamentary Debates* (Commons), December 5, 1984, p. 399.

3. *South China Morning Post*, September 27, 1984.

4. *Ming Pao*, September 27, 1984.

5. Kevin Rafferty, *City on the Rocks* (London: Viking Press, 1989), p. 441.

6. Lydia Dunn, "Motion on the Draft Agreement on the Future of Hong Kong," Legislative Council, October 15, 1984.

7. Frank Ching, *Hong Kong and China: For Better or For Worse* (New York: The Asia Society, 1985), p. 44.

8. Rafferty, *City on the Rocks*, p. 442.

9. Emily Lau, "Drawing Up Lines," *Far Eastern Economic Review*, October 25, 1984, p. 19.

10. Report of the Assessment Office, *Arrangements for testing the acceptability in Hong Kong of the Draft Agreement on the Future of the Territory* (Hong Kong: Government Printing Office, Nov. 29, 1984), vol. II.

11. "No cheering over Hong Kong," *The Economist*, September 22–28, 1984.

12. Lau, "Drawing Up Lines," p. 18.

13. John Walden, *Excellency, Your Gap Is Growing!* (Hong Kong: All Noble Co., 1987), p. 69.

14. Report of the Assessment Office, sec. 3.22.

15. Ibid., sec. 3.23.

16. Ibid., sec. 4.66.

17. Ibid., sec. 3.25.

18. Ibid., sec. 4.67.

19. Ibid., sec. 3.1.

20. *Green Paper: The Future Development of Representative Government in Hong Kong* (Hong Kong: Government Printing Office, July 1984), sec. 1.

21. Ibid.

22. Great Britain, *Hansard's Parliamentary Debates* (Commons), July 18, 1984, p. 201.

23. Sir Edward Youde, *Address to the Legislative Council*, September 1984.

24. Sir Edward Youde, *Annual Address to the Legislative Council*, October 4, 1984.

25. *White Paper: The Further Development of Representative Government in Hong Kong* (Hong Kong: Government Printing Office, November 1984.

26. Great Britain, *Hansard's Parliamentary Debates* (Commons), December 5, 1984, p. 464.

27. Ibid., p. 470.

28. Great Britain, *Hansard's Parliamentary Debates* (Lords), December 10, 1984, p. 85.

29. *Annual Report on Hong Kong to Parliament 1985–86* (London: Government Printing Office, 1987).

30. "Appraisal of Surveys and Other Material Relating to the 1987 Review of Developments of Representative Government in Hong Kong," quoted in William McGurn, ed., *Basic Law, Basic Questions* (Hong Kong: Review Publishing Co., 1988), p. 160.

31. *White Paper on the Development of Representative Government: The Way Forward* (Hong Kong: Government Printing Office, February 1988), sec. 28.

32. Sir David Wilson, "The Future of the Crown Colony," *Harvard International Review*, November 1987.

33. Peter Tsao, *Hong Kong Hansard's Session 1987/88*, May 4, 1988, p. 1318.

34. Paul C. K. Kwong, "Population and Immigration," in T. L. Tsim and Bernard H. K. Luk, eds., *The Other Hong Kong Report* (Hong Kong: Chinese University Press, 1989), p. 378.

35. Ibid., p. 379.

36. Michael Bociurkiw, "More women fly out to give babies foreign citizenship," *South China Morning Post*, November 25, 1990.

37. Danny Gittings, "Soviet base proposes a new Hong Kong," *South China Morning Post*, November 25, 1990.

38. Simon Macklin and Bernard Fong, "More professionals queue up to join brain drain," *South China Morning Post*, February 1, 1989.

39. William McGurn, "Boat People in Guccis," *The International Economy*, September/October 1989, p. 85.

CHAPTER FOUR

1. Robert Adley, *All Change Hong Kong* (Dorset, England: Blanford Press, 1984), p. 114.

2. Great Britain, *Hansard's Parliamentary Debates* (Commons), January 20, 1988, pp. 1005–6.

3. Jane McCartney, "The Students," in George Hicks, ed., *The Broken Mirror* (London: Longman Group, 1990), p. 8.

4. John Greenwald, "Next Door and Eight Years Away," *Time*, June 5, 1989.

5. McCartney, "The Students," p. 17.

6. "Troops in scuffle with students," *South China Morning Post*, June 3, 1989.

7. "Beijing slaughter will force drastic changes," *South China Morning Post*, June 5, 1989.

8. Joseph Cheng, "Prospects for Democracy in Hong Kong," in Hicks, *The Broken Mirror*, p. 282.

9. *China Daily*, June 12, 1989; quoted by Frank Ching, "Red Star Over Hong Kong," *World Policy Journal*, Fall 1989, p. 659.

10. Associated Press, "China Warns Hong Kong Residents," *Washington Post*, July 22, 1989.

11. Antony Acland, "A Future for Hong Kong," *Washington Times*, May 26, 1990.

12. Michael Chugani, "1997 jitters 'blown out of proportion,'" *South China Morning Post*, May 24, 1990.

13. "Still confident says Thatcher," *Hongkong Standard*, June 5, 1989.

14. Ibid.

15. "Current Events in China," statement by Sir Geoffrey to the House of Commons, June 6, 1989.

16. Fox Butterfield, "British Foreign Secretary Booed by Angry Crowds in Hong Kong," *New York Times*, July 3, 1989.

17. Charles Moore, "Fiddling While Freedom Fades," *The Spectator*, November 25, 1989, p. 11.

18. Emily Lau, "Cadres and Criminals," *Far Eastern Economic Review*, May 24, 1990.

19. "Uncertain Rights," *Far Eastern Economic Review*, July 4, 1991, p. 16.

20. Barbara Basler, "Few in Hong Kong Ask to Be British," *New York Times*, March 1, 1991.

21. Philip Bowring and Emily Lau, "Without a Fight," *Far Eastern Economic Review*, February 1, 1990, p. 18.

CHAPTER FIVE

1. Great Britain, *Hansard's Parliamentary Debates* (Commons), December 5, 1984, p. 435.

2. Ibid. p. 460.

3. Ibid. p. 470.

4. Ibid. p. 464.

5. Figures relating to U.S. trade with and business involvement in the colony have been supplied by the American Chamber of Commerce in Hong Kong.

Bibliography

Adley, Robert. *All Change Hong Kong*. Poole, Dorset, England: Blanford Press, 1984.

All About Shanghai: A Standard Guidebook. Shanghai: University Press, 1934–35. Hong Kong: Oxford University Press, 1983.

Barber, Noel. *The Fall of Shanghai*. New York: Coward, McCann & Geoghegan, 1979.

Bonavia, David. *The Chinese*. New York: Lippincott & Crowell, 1980.

————. *Hong Kong 1997: The Final Settlement*. Hong Kong: South China Morning Post, 1985.

Butterfield, Fox. *China: Alive in the Bitter Sea*. 2nd ed. New York: Random House, 1990.

Cheng, Joseph Y. S., ed. *Hong Kong: In Search of a Future*. Hong Kong: Oxford University Press, 1984.

Cheng, Nien. *Life and Death in Shanghai*. New York: Grove Press, 1986.

Ching, Frank. *Hong Kong and China: For Better or For Worse*. New York: The Asia Society, 1985.

Chiu, Hungdah, Jao, Y. C., and Wu, Yuan-Li. *The Future of Hong Kong: Toward 1997 and Beyond*. Westport, Conn.: Quorum Books, 1987.

Emmons, Charles F. *Hong Kong Prepares for 1997: Politics and Emigration in 1987*. Hong Kong: Centre of Asian Studies, University of Hong Kong, 1988.

Endacott, G. B. *A Short History of Hong Kong*. 2nd ed. Hong Kong: Oxford University Press, 1988.

Hicks, George, ed. *The Broken Mirror: China After Tiananmen*. London: Longman Group, 1990.

Hughes, Richard. *Borrowed Place, Borrowed Time: Hong Kong and Its Many Faces*. 2nd ed. Singapore: Toppan Publishing Co., 1976.

Kelly, Ian. *Hong Kong: A Political-Geographic Analysis*. Honolulu: University of Hawaii Press, 1986.

Kelly and Walsh. *The Hong Kong Guide 1893*. 2nd ed. Hong Kong: Oxford University Press, 1982.

Keswick, Maggie. *The Thistle and the Jade: A Celebration of 150 Years of Jardine, Matheson & Co*. London: Octopus Books, 1982.

Lau, Siu-Kai, and Kuan, Hsin-Chi. *The Ethos of the Hong Kong Chinese*. 2nd printing. Hong Kong: Chinese University Press, 1989.

Ling, Pan. *In Search of Old Shanghai*. Hong Kong: Joint Publishing Co., 1982.

Mann, Richard I. *Business in Hong Kong: Signposts for the '90s, A Positive View*. Toronto: Gateway Books, 1990.

Mattock, Katherine. *This Is Hong Kong: The Story of Government House*. 2nd ed. Hong Kong: Government Information Services, 1979.

Mason, Richard. *The World of Suzie Wong*. London: Collins, 1957.

McGurn, William, ed. *Basic Law, Basic Questions: The Debate Continues*. Hong Kong: Review Publishing Co., 1988.

Morris, Jan. *Hong Kong: Xianggang*. New York: Viking Press, 1989.

Patrikeeff, Felix. *Mouldering Pearl: Hong Kong at the Crossroads*. London: George Philip, 1989.

Rabushka, Alvin. *The New China: Comparative Economic Development in Mainland China, Taiwan, and Hong Kong*. San Francisco: Pacific Research Institute for Public Policy, 1987.

Rafferty, Kevin. *City on the Rocks: Hong Kong's Uncertain Future*. New York: Viking Press, 1989.

Scott, Ian. *Political Change and the Crisis of Legitimacy in Hong Kong*. Honolulu: University of Hawaii Press, 1989.

Spence, Jonathan D. *The Search for Modern China*. New York: W. W. Norton and Co., 1990.

Tsim, T. L., and Luk, Bernard H. K., eds. *The Other Hong Kong Report*. Hong Kong: Chinese University Press, 1989.

Wacks, Raymond. *Civil Liberties in Hong Kong*. Hong Kong: Oxford University Press, 1988.

Walden, John. *Excellency, Your Gap Is Growing! Six Talks on a Chinese Takeaway*. Hong Kong: All Noble Co., 1987.

————. *Excellency, Your Gap Is Showing! Six Critiques on British Colonial Government in Hong Kong.* Hong Kong: Corporate Communications, 1983.

Williams, Stephanie. *Hongkong Bank: The Building of Norman Foster's Masterpiece.* Boston: Little Brown and Co., 1989.

Wiltshire, Trea. *Hong Kong: An Impossible Journey Through History.* Rev. ed. Hong Kong: Serasia, 1987.

Yee, Albert. *A People Misruled: Hong Kong and the Chinese Stepping Stone Syndrome.* Hong Kong: API Press, 1989.

PERIODICALS—*Asian Wall Street Journal. Far Eastern Economic Review. Hansard's Parliamentary Debates. South China Morning Post.*

Index of Names

159